All Relationships

Inevitably End

A Much Needed Conversation

NOLAN BLAKE

All Relationships Inevitably End
A Much Needed Conversation

Copyright © 2021 Nolan Blake

All rights reserved. No part of this book may be reproduced or used in any way or manner whatsoever without written permission from the copyright owner, except for the use of quotations embodied in critical articles and reviews. For more information, email AuthorNolanBlake@gmail.com.

Publisher's Cataloging-in-Publication data
Names: Blake, Nolan, author.
Title: All relationships inevitably end : a much needed conversation / Nolan Blake.
Description: New York, NY: Nolan Blake, 2022.
Identifiers: LCCN: 2021919495
ISBN: 978-1-7378848-0-4 (paperback)
978-1-7378848-1-1 (hardcover)
978-1-7378848-2-8 (ebook)
978-1-7378848-3-5 (audio)
Subjects: LCSH Dating (Social customs). | Marriage. Relationships. | BISAC FAMILY & RELATIONSHIPS / Dating FAMILY & RELATIONSHIPS / Marriage & Long-Term Relationships FAMILY & RELATIONSHIPS / Love &Romance
Classification: LCC HQ801 .B53 2022 | DDC 306.7--dc23

Nolan Blake
90 Vermilyea Ave Suite 294,
New York, NY, 10034

www.NolanBlake.net

To everyone that wants a love that is untethered to time, truly unconditional and pure.

Table of Contents

Introduction 7
Prologue 9
    Three Important Factors 11
    Chemistry: First Impressions and Beyond 12
    Days, Months, Years: The Path to Growth 14
    Experience: How We are Shaped 16
    Challenging Concepts Open Doors To New
    Discoveries & Ideas 18
    Why All This Matters 19
Chemistry 21
    What Does Chemistry Mean? 23
    Chemistry Factor #1: Context 25
    Chemistry Factor #2: Personality 29
    Chemistry Factor #3: Serendipity 32
    Chemistry vs. True Love? 35
    Chemistry: After the Honeymoon 38
    The Conclusion of Chemistry 45
    Obligation vs. Inspiration 49
    Representatives 51
Growth 54
    Happily Ever After? 56
    Ongoing Opportunities 57
    Individual Growth vs. Relationship Growth 66
    Relationship Stages 67
    When and Where You Are 77
Experience 82
    Time: Friend or Foe? 83

Fixed and Moving Actions 84
Passive and Active Experience 87
Charting Your Experience 90
Experiencing Life Together 94
Experiencing the End 96
Live or Let Die 102
What Are We? 103
Happiness 104
Cheating 111
What Is Cheating? 113
Who Cheats? 116
The Excuses 118
Cheating: Risks and Impact 119
Cheating in an "Open" Relationship 124
Cheating and Growth 125
Sexualized Bodies 131
Social Media 132
The Sexualization of Women 133
Exaggerated Differences 136
Achieving the Appearance You Want 138
Appearance as Empowerment 139
Therapy 143
Help From the Outside 144
The Professionals 146
Reaching a Shared Understanding 148
Vicious Cycles 149
A Theory of Change 152
Dating Websites 154
Ease of Access 155
What's Missing From Dating Apps 156
Sexual Gratification 158

Playing the Game 159
How Open Is Too Open? 161
Because you Have Nothing Better To Do 162
Experience Is What It's All About **165**
Choose Wisely 169
Experiences Last a Lifetime 172
About the Author **174**

Introduction

If the title of this book hasn't turned you away, then you are likely a person who has experienced challenges in your relationships or dating life. So much of the suffering people face stems from other people, so why do we even bother? We invest so much in others because we expect a return, but we often ignore the fact that this is not guaranteed. A person is not an asset that guarantees a return. It isn't cynical to say that all relationships end. It is a fact. This book is about acknowledging and accepting hard facts as a way to grow while getting more satisfaction and joy from relationships.

Although all relationships do end, this book will help you view your relationship more objectively, navigate and resolve conflict, and hopefully provide some perspective to extend the life of your relationship. By the same token, this book provides insights and opportunities for reflection that can help you bring a relationship to a conclusion that preserves the dignity and well-being of everyone involved. Too often, relationships don't end until people get hurt, but this is not a foregone conclusion. The end of a relationship can be gentle, loving, even an act of kindness and compassion.

Rather than read this book cover to cover, you may choose to check the table of contents and navigate to the section most applicable to your current situation. As things change, jump around and read more. There is also benefit to be gained from reading a chapter more than once. Consider reading a section or two at random. You may find an insight or a question that prompts you to reflect on your current situation in a surprising and illuminating way.

I hope you enjoy the book. I hope it will spark debate, both internally and with your partners past, present and future. Incorporating these ideas into your relationship outlook will lead to an open mind and a heightened ability to arrive objectively at constructive conclusions to conflicts large and small. Reading this book is a proactive step towards a more fulfilling and joyful relationship.

Prologue

Every new beginning is a cause for celebration. We celebrate the start of the new year by gathering with friends and loved ones. We celebrate each birth as the beginning of a new life. We celebrate the start of a new job, the first night in a new home, the new union symbolized by marriage.

Have you ever considered why we instinctively mark every beginning with some kind of ritual? The answer is hope.

Hope is the psychological and emotional equivalent of food or water. It sustains us. It motivates us. It allows us to persevere through the many challenges and pitfalls of modern life. Hope comes with every new beginning, so it makes sense that we celebrate.

For a book titled *All Relationships Inevitably End,* it may seem counterintuitive to focus on the nature of beginnings. After all, this is a pessimistic book intended to convince you that relationships aren't worth the trouble, right? Not quite.

This book is about how relationships start, how they are sustained, and yes, how they may conclude. The simple premise "all relationships end" is not meant as a condemnation of all relationships. Far from it.

This book takes the rational view that a relationship is just like any other system or organism. No one lives forever. No job lasts forever. No moment of suffering in this life lasts forever. These truths may be difficult to talk about, but what do we gain by ignoring them? Why should the impermanence of a relationship—and by extension, life—prevent you from feeling fully loved and fulfilled?

If you've ever been in a relationship, you are familiar with the feeling of hope that comes with the first moment of connection. Perhaps you are in a relationship now, and you still feel the warmth of hope in your heart. In either case, it seems counterintuitive to spend even a moment worrying about how things might go wrong.

Society has conditioned many of us to believe that it is somehow a sign of weakness to even think about it. This book will show that *acknowledging* the fact that every relationship will end is not at all the same as *worrying* about it. Worrying is a waste of time.

Acknowledgment is one of the greatest gifts you can give yourself and the ones you love.

Perhaps the celebration of a new beginning has another purpose beyond the embrace of hope. Maybe it provides us a useful distraction from a darkness that sits just out of view. When we celebrate a beginning, we can pretend, just for a little while, that our feeling of hope will last forever.

When you embark on a new journey, the last thing you want to think about is how that journey will end but thinking about it will remind you to embrace it while it's still happening. It doesn't feel good to spend time worrying about what might go wrong. Everyone tells you to live in the moment. The past is over, the future is uncertain, and all you have is the present, right?

There is a fine line between worrying about the future and acknowledging the certainty of every beginning's end. The future isn't set in stone. It is up to each one of us to write the story of our lives. However, it is often beyond your control to dictate when and how that story ends. This may seem like a dark thought, but the real danger comes when you ignore it.

Worrying about the future is not the same as recognizing this fact: All things, good or bad, will come to an end. Every job, every relationship and every life will end one way or the other.

This book takes as a given what many "self-help" books about relationships fail to even acknowledge: All relationships inevitably end. It's possible to keep this fact in mind while also getting the most possible joy and fulfillment out of your relationship, no matter what stage it is in. The goal is to get couples to extend the life of their relationships by doing what's best for themselves and their partner.

Three Important Factors

You don't need a whole book to acknowledge the simple fact that all relationships end. Those three words could fit on a bumper sticker. The truth is, understanding the impermanence of relationships is only the first step. Keep in mind that it isn't enough just to say the words out loud. *All relationships end* is not a magical incantation. It won't help you feel more secure in your relationship and it won't help you find love. Not without a few other ingredients.

It is worth pausing here to say that this book will benefit anyone truly interested in getting the most out of their relationship. For those who find themselves single—whether by choice or not—this book will help you identify the traits to look for a future partner. Too often, what you think you want and what you need in a partner are two different things.

This book focuses on three factors that together provide a roadmap for navigating the complexities of relationships in today's world: chemistry, growth and experience. It is important to understand that these three factors are inevitable aspects of human life. We all feel a certain chemistry when we meet another person. We all live lives that are full of experiences that we ascribe meaning to. And, we all grow. Let's take a quick look at each of these concepts before diving in.

Chemistry: First Impressions and Beyond

Think about the last time you met a new person. Were you introduced by a friend or did you meet them on your own? Did you meet them randomly or through a dating app? These factors are more important than you might think.

Conventional wisdom says that first impressions matter, but how much? Research in psychology has produced evidence of a phenomenon called the "halo effect." Simply put, a positive first impression acts like a halo—it casts a glow over every part of your personality. That "halo" will prime other people to seek out your other positive qualities.

By contrast, a negative first impression could make it harder for people to see your good qualities. For example, showing up late to a job interview may put you at a disadvantage. To many people, tardiness is not a good thing. A potential employer may count lateness as a strike against you. This doesn't mean that you won't get the job, but it does mean you may have to work harder to prove yourself.

The same goes for relationships. Dating is challenging because you don't really know what the other person is looking for. You might think that showing up in a suit and tie or a fancy dress would make a positive first impression. However, the other person might think you are too stuffy and proper. Navigating first impressions is an important part of understanding the chemistry you have with a potential partner.

Of course, relationships are not just about first impressions. Chemistry is something that can be cultivated over time, and it isn't static. Anyone who has ever moved in with a person they have been dating for a while knows how different things can be when you share a home. Each partner needs to establish new boundaries, and this can alter a relationship's chemistry.

When you enter a relationship, you must be prepared for these kinds of changes. If you and your partner understand the chemistry of your relationship, it will be much easy to resolve conflicts when they arise.

Chemistry also goes hand in hand with compatibility. How many times have you met someone and thought, "How could anyone want to be in a relationship with this person?" Sometimes, you encounter people who possess traits that really turn you off. Unless this trait is based on your prejudice, there is no need to feel guilty. You just don't have good chemistry with this person. Still, an important goal of this book is to encourage you to keep an open mind.

Sometimes, it can take a while for a person to show you their truest self. Perhaps you are one of these people. Perhaps you don't see the value in laying all your cards on the table right away. This is a completely reasonable way to be. When meeting new people, keeping an open mind is so important. Remember, the halo effect is an observed psychological phenomenon, but it isn't destiny. It is almost always beneficial to question the assumptions you make about other people.

However, sometimes the chemistry just isn't there. Countless relationships never got off the ground because of a lack of chemistry. A person who isn't right for you may be perfect for someone else. In the chapter titled "Chemistry," we'll look at the various types of chemistry that can exist between two people. Then, we'll analyze the ways this chemistry can develop over time. Understanding the type of chemistry you have with your partner—and the type of chemistry you need—will be the first step in cultivating or maintaining a healthy relationship.

Days, Months, Years: The Path to Growth

The second factor that this book is concerned with is growth. You probably associate growth with the physical changes that you experienced as you transitioned from child to adult, but it happens throughout life, whether you feel it or not. Perhaps you have fond memories of the growth chart your parents kept on the wall. Every few months, you would stand and mark the change in your height.

Growth is a sign of development. It is a sign that you are moving forward, destined for bigger and better things. But, in the context of a relationship, growth can be a frightening prospect. Even though physical growth typically ends in adolescence, all humans continue to develop intellectually and emotionally, usually in response to life changes.

We all know someone who just seems "stuck" in life. Stuck in a job they hate, stuck with a partner they don't love, perhaps stuck in the home where they grew up. It is easy to pass judgment on these people, but appearances can sometimes be deceiving. Someone may not be actively changing their life, but they may be planning, thinking and responding to their circumstances as best they can. We should all try to have a bit more compassion for those who we are inclined to judge.

Growth is frightening because it is often followed by change. Any threat to the status quo poses unique challenges and opportunities. In the context of a relationship, growth is particularly troublesome because individuals never grow at the same rate. One partner may be pursuing a path of self-betterment: getting an education, hunting for a new job, embarking on a new fitness regimen. The other partner may be perfectly content with the way things are. Neither one is better than the other, but you can see how growth can lead to conflict in such a situation.

If you recognize that all forms of growth carry the potential to end a relationship—even a happy one—you will be better poised to handle such challenges with honesty. How might you respond to the growth of your partner? Are you willing to support the growth of your partner, even if such growth puts a strain on other parts of your relationship?

The chapter titled "Growth" will tackle these questions head-on. We'll dissect the different types of growth that people and relationships can experience. For better or worse, growth is an inevitable part of the human condition. What matters is how you respond to it.

Experience: How We are Shaped

Experience, the third and final factor, is the most crucial. Growth and experience may be closely related, but they have very different implications. Let's take a moment to analyze the distinction.

Some experiences are the product of your *agency*—when you exercise a choice. You choose which cereal to buy at the grocery store in the same way that you choose which people to let into your life. Some choices come with much higher stakes than others.

While each decision you make comes with specific pros and cons, there is no way to know what the consequences will be. This is why it is sometimes very difficult to make sense of your experiences. "Why did I do/say that?" you might ask yourself after an argument with a loved one. But, exercising your agency only leads to one kind of experience. Some experiences are just the natural consequences of things beyond your control.

Where you go to school, work and live are all factors that impact the kinds of experiences you have. The more resources you have, the greater the variety of experiences available to you. However, experience does not necessarily translate to growth, and this is why this book makes a clear distinction between these two factors. Here is an illustration:

You might have heard stories of Buddhist monks reaching enlightenment after years of solitary meditation. These individuals have very little by way of traditional experience—they haven't traveled extensively, they haven't interacted with people from different walks of life, they don't read the news—yet their minds have grown to encompass greater understanding than most of us can achieve in a lifetime. Lacking the resources for a life rich in varied experience is hardly an excuse to not focus on growth.

Sometimes, experiences can surprise you. You can spend months agonizing over which TV set to buy, only to find yourself disappointed when it finally arrives. You might hit traffic even though your GPS told you the roads were clear. A throwaway date can lead to a lifelong relationship.

The world is a chaotic place, yet you spend countless hours trying to make sense of the experiences you have. This is what it means to live a human life. Humans have the cognitive ability to wonder about our circumstances, yet we often lack the insight to truly understand them. However, this does not mean that you should throw up your hands and accept the randomness of fate.

Making sense of your experiences isn't entirely futile. Putting forth a consistent effort to understand and make meaning from what life throws your way is an invaluable part of building a strong relationship. When you make decisions thoughtfully and interpret the results logically, you show others that you care about how your actions affect them.

In the context of a romantic relationship, your actions, whether you intend them to or not, have a direct impact on your partner. It isn't realistic to ask permission every time you make a decision. Instead, set boundaries and communicate often about your hopes and goals for the future. Tough conversations don't always need to be negative in tone. This idea will recur several times in this book, not just the "Experience" chapter.

A distinct but overlapping kind of experience is what you share with your partner. A couple that shares meaningful experiences build a common understanding of the world. This is why people always warn you about going on a trip with someone you just met. Navigating new experiences with a new person is full of pitfalls.

However, this doesn't mean you shouldn't take these kinds of chances. The chapter on experience will, among other things, discuss how to make meaning out of your own experiences as well as those you share with your partner.

Challenging Concepts Open Doors To New Discoveries & Ideas

If any of the ideas presented in this introduction make you uncomfortable, ask yourself why. Why is it so hard to accept the idea that all relationships end? Why is it so difficult to acknowledge the fact of death as the ultimate end awaiting each one of us? Why is it so difficult to accept that you do not have full control over your destiny?

Everyone finds different answers to these very difficult questions. Most of us grow up in a world where personal responsibility is the highest moral value. Only the individual is responsible for their lot in life. On a practical level and a public policy level, this makes sense. If everyone looks out for themselves, then society should chug smoothly along like a train on its tracks.

Unfortunately, this idea simply does not hold 100% of the time. Sometimes, life is beyond our control. Accepting this is one of the keys to relationship longevity.

Why All This Matters

You might be wondering what you stand to gain by acknowledging that all relationships inevitably end. Isn't it pessimistic? How does this make you a better relationship partner? Again, the past is over, the future hasn't happened, all we have is the present, right? Exactly.

To make the most out of the present moment, we cannot shy away from the fact that all relationships inevitably end. Likewise, we cannot shy away from the fact that we aren't always fully in control of how life develops. When you enter into a relationship, you are, in a sense, agreeing to cede some control to your partner. Your life ceases to be fully yours because relationships require compromise to function.

If you need to be fully in control at every waking moment, if you refuse to take the lived experience of others into account, then you have no business partaking in relationships of any kind. Being in a relationship means knowing when to give up control. It means accepting that other people are just as flawed, just as confused and just as uncertain about the future as you are. If you refuse to acknowledge life's inconvenient realities, you run the risk of holding yourself, and your partner, to impossible standards.

But this book is more than questions, it is a roadmap to answers. By understanding the implications of chemistry, growth and experience, you position yourself to be a more reliable and grateful person. You become the kind of person that is truly capable of caring for others in a meaningful way. You will be able to enjoy your life instead of regretting the past, critiquing the present and worrying about the future.

At the end of the day, everyone wants to feel content and grateful for the life they have, even if things aren't ideal. When given the choice, wouldn't you choose happiness?

Chemistry

"With everyone you meet, you experience a different kind of chemistry."

The world is full of mysteries, far too many to solve in a single lifetime. Think of how many mysteries you encounter just on a normal day. If you're like most people in the developed world, the first thing you do in the morning is grab your phone and check your messages. How often do you think about how your phone actually works? What is the battery made of? How does it provide power? How do your photos and messages travel through the air, sometimes for thousands of miles, before reaching their destination? How does Wi-Fi work? How does your touchscreen work? How about facial recognition?

Think about this another way. If civilization were somehow reset, how long would it take you to build an iPhone? Would you know which raw materials to extract from the ground and where to find them? Would you be able to process those materials and mold them into the proper shape? Would you be able to harness enough energy and knowledge to build the microchips necessary to store all the required information? Could you devise and program the codes and algorithms necessary for even the most basic app?

Even if you answered "yes" to one or more of the questions, there is likely not a single person in the entire world who could build an iPhone—or any smartphone—from scratch, and this makes perfect sense. It is often said that humans are social creatures. We require partnership, community and collaboration to reach our full potential. When you interact with others, you have the potential to generate ideas and perspectives that you otherwise could not.

Human collaboration has produced the wonders of modern technology. It has produced innovations in the food we consume, the clothes we wear, the way we transport ourselves and goods. The same holds true for our relationships. Friendship, intimacy and bonds of family allow us to innovate our lives. Strong relationships make us better, wiser and more able to face the challenges of daily life. By the same token, toxic relationships can handicap us, weaken us and fill us with false ideas about ourselves and the world.

This chapter will attempt to illuminate what happens when two people come together to build something new. It breaks down and analyzes how strangers become partners in the hopes of reaching helpful conclusions about the nature of human chemistry.

This chapter will illuminate the various ways that two people come together to build something new. It breaks down how chemistry is a main factor that will have a huge impact on your relationship. After understanding how chemistry works, you will be better equipped when you face the strains of chemistry and its effects over time. You will reach a helpful conclusion about the nature of human chemistry.

There are roughly 7.5 billion people in the world (2018 figure). An average person living in a city or suburb will encounter around 80,000 people in a lifetime. That is only an infinitesimal fraction of the total world population. With everyone you meet, you experience a different kind of chemistry.

When you consider the fact that you will have unique chemistry with every person you meet, the possibilities for the many different experiences you can have are staggering and profound. The mind cannot possibly grasp what it would mean to get to know that many people in a single lifetime. Thankfully, this isn't the issue at hand.

What Does Chemistry Mean?

The very word, chemistry, itself has an origin steeped in mystery. The modern English word "chemistry" evolved from the word "alchemy." Today, we associate "alchemy" with the mystical quest to turn lead into gold, but early alchemists were also concerned with philosophy, astronomy and the study of the physical world. Going back even further in history, many believe that the origin of the word alchemy is the Arabic term "el-Kimia," which comes from the Greek for "cast together."

Today, chemistry is recognized as the scientific discipline concerned with the elements as well as more complex compounds. In the traditional sense, a chemist is interested in what happens when two or more compounds react. Understanding this history should make it easy to see why the world also came to describe the particular "reaction" that occurs when two people meet for the first time.

Next time you meet someone new, try and notice the feelings that arise. Even if this is just a cashier or someone working at the fast-food drive-through. Does the person make you feel a certain way? Relaxed? Irritated? Somewhere in the middle?

After the interaction, try to figure out why you had the reaction you did. Were you already in a bad or good mood? Did the person say something or perhaps speak in a particular tone of voice?

More likely than not, your reaction had something to do with their appearance. Whether you realize it, most of us make immediate judgments based simply on how another person looks, how they are dressed and how they carry themselves.

Once you get into the habit of noticing your reactions to those around you, you will be more attuned to your biases. Everyone has biases, and many people can admit to themselves what their biases are. The hard part is overcoming your bias. This doesn't mean eliminating your bias altogether—this is nearly impossible. Instead, your goal should be to understand how your bias impacts your feelings towards other people.

Chemistry is really nothing but a feeling. As with all feelings, they can lead us down many paths. To give yourself the best chance of finding someone with the right chemistry for you, you first need to confront your own biases. Otherwise, you might walk away from a great match, and no one wants to spend their life wondering "what if."

Your bias is something that only you can address, but other elements affect chemistry. Let's spend some time looking at these other factors.

Chemistry Factor #1: Context

"The experiences we have shape the way we are."

How and where you meet a person matters almost as much as the person. Context and other background information help you set expectations. As you are likely already aware, expectations are a major factor in maintaining the health and longevity of a relationship. You might not know that expectations play a role before you even meet a new person.

Let's say that your friend or co-worker is setting you up on a blind date. Maybe they tell you all about the person, or maybe you do your own social media sleuthing to figure out who you are about to meet. Either way, it is tough to argue that the date is actually "blind." When you meet a person online or through an app—unless it's for a hookup—you probably took the time to learn a bit about them through messaging. You might want to know things like what they do for work, what they do in their spare time, what their likes and dislikes are and what their goals for the future are. While the answers to these questions can give you a sense of who this person is, they might also mislead you into making assumptions about a person.

Even in contemporary times, most romantic relationships begin as friendships. This type of context is very different from a "blind date" or matching with someone on an app. Couples who begin relationships as friends face unique challenges, especially in terms of chemistry. There is no telling how the chemistry between friends will change once they become romantically involved. Being honest about your expectations could help mitigate some of these challenges.

Meeting through mutual friends is another common way for a relationship to start. In these cases, two people already share a context, which can help them get past the "getting to know you" phase a bit quicker. Again, the danger here lies in making assumptions. You might think you understand the chemistry you have with this person and perhaps you've even spent time together in the past. Unfortunately, a romantic attachment can change everything.

When you meet someone new, consider how the specific context of your meeting is affecting the way you see them. Even if the person is familiar to you, take time at the outset to ask what they want out of a relationship. Such a simple question can really help a relationship get off on the right foot. Such a question may also prompt a budding relationship to end. You might not want to celebrate such a disappointment, but it is better than the alternative: learning too late that you have an irreconcilable difference with your partner.

The way you interact with each person creates an experience that is one of a kind. It is based on the chemistry you both bring out of each other. There are so many people in the world and we are all so very different, but we do share some similarities. You can meet someone that reminds you of someone else, but that experience is still very unique.

When you're in a relationship and you're experiencing one type of chemistry, you will get used to it over time. We are creatures that feel most alive on new adventures and experiences. Going on vacation takes a while to get old because every time you go on one, it is a new adventure.

In general, you know what to expect when traveling but it's the different people you meet each time and being in a new location that makes the vacation different, special and unique. The thought of going on a vacation will always be an adventure due to its unique experience. We all live for experiences whether it's being in the moment, embarking on a journey to accomplish a goal or even just relaxing.

There are some people who bring out the adventurous side of you, some that bring out your silliness and others that bring out a better version of yourself. We like to experience new things and we are constantly growing and evolving as individuals.

When people are in a relationship, over time most of those individuals feel like they're not living life anymore or the relationship is getting boring. They may blame each other and fight about it, but they don't realize it isn't either of their faults. They are essentially experiencing one type of chemistry. If the person isn't right for you, it doesn't take long to feel like you're over them and that situation. The relationship can last longer, but no matter what, chemistry will always remain as one of the main factors that ends relationships.

Even if that person is right for you, you will, unfortunately, eventually get used to your relationship. But this feeling will come sooner if the person isn't right for you at all. It will not take long for you to be over that type of chemistry. This is why people always stress waiting for the "right person." The right person does not have to be your true love. There are multiple people who are your true loves, yes, plural, and there are people that you are compatible with.

If you meet someone that you're compatible with, you can still have a long-lasting relationship with that person. Your true loves may have more things in common with you, but the person you are compatible with has common interests as well. The relationship will require a little more effort to stay together, but if you both want the relationship to work, whether they're your true love or not, it will.

The reason why relationships will inevitably fail based on chemistry is that as humans, we like to experience life. We get used to certain routines and when we do, we need to change them out of boredom and for our sanity and entertainment. When we're in a relationship with someone that we only experience one kind of chemistry, we begin to feel as though we are missing something or somehow missing out on life. This happens because we become used to our significant other and the dynamic of the relationship.

Eventually, after doing so many things together, it is going to be the same routine relationship, just a different day. No more surprises, spontaneity or new experiences unless you both make the effort to add new experiences. Many couples still function well and are happy with their routine. They wouldn't want to get to know anyone else and after being together for years, I wouldn't want that either.

Why leave the one you're with to run the risk of being with someone new that you have no idea how they'll treat you or how much you may, or may not, get along? The couples that last for years understand the key to staying together. The key is that they want to stay together even through all the ups and downs. As for the couples that lack the desire for one another and the interest to stay together, it's not so easy.

Chemistry Factor #2: Personality

"What was once brand new and exciting has now become routine."

Those who study the discipline of psychology have come up with countless ways of identifying and categorizing personality types. These ideas can be informative, but they can just as easily mislead people into forming unrealistic expectations about their romantic prospects and the health of their relationships.

In fact, there is very little evidence that personality "types" even exist. The very idea has fallen out of favor with many psychologists. For this reason, it may be foolish to put too much stock in tests or quizzes that purport to place a person in a single personality bucket. People are far more complex and any attempt to reduce people into neat categories will ultimately fail. Most personality tests, including the popular Myers-Briggs Type Indicator, acknowledges that all types exist on a continuum. Everyone possesses traits that fall into multiple personality types. Some just have more than others.

Instead of thinking in terms of personality types, it helps to think in terms of traits. A trait is just a characteristic that a person is likely to display. Everyone displays multiple traits and people with very different personalities can express the same trait. For example, two people might share the trait of staying calm under pressure, but in a low-pressure situation, they might behave very differently.

When it comes to chemistry, personality traits combine in unpredictable ways. The first step is to understand your own personality traits. This is often more challenging than identifying the traits in others. Your own biases often prevent you from seeing and acknowledging traits that you aren't proud of or comfortable with.

The Big Five Personality Traits model emerged in the 1980s and continues to be studied and developed today. It uses massive quantities of survey data to describe five distinct dimensions of personality. Think of each dimension as a continuum that every person falls on. Someone who goes skydiving, for example, may be more resilient and confident in certain ways than a person who prefers golfing.

Keep in mind that you should not draw conclusions from just one or two facts about a person. A person with the confidence to skydive, for example, may crumble under the pressure of having to give a public speech. Context plays an important role in how your personality expresses itself.

Each of the Big Five personality types is a continuum. Everyone falls somewhere in the range of each factor. The five factors include:

- **Openness to experience:** Inventive/curious vs. consistent/cautious
- **Conscientiousness:** Efficient/organized vs. extravagant/careless
- **Extraversion:** Outgoing/energetic vs. solitary/reserved
- **Agreeableness:** Friendly/compassionate vs. challenging/callous
- **Neuroticism:** Sensitive/nervous vs. resilient/confident

If you can develop a general understanding of your own personality traits, then you are better equipped to describe yourself honestly to others. Likewise, if you take the time to understand the traits of your potential partner, you stand the greatest chance of setting reasonable expectations.

There are several tools that you can use to ascertain where you land on each of the Big Five dimensions. Most of us have been guilty of having expectations for other people and when it turns out they don't meet that expectation, there is disappointment followed by many other emotions.

Recall that chemistry is about reactions. It's about what happens when two people get together, acting and reacting to one another in real-time. When you combine an understanding of the context of the meeting and the personality traits of each person, you stand the greatest chance of making sense of the chemistry.

If chemistry is built incorrectly, it's difficult to do anything new in your relationship because of the way you both have shaped your relationship.

Sometimes being spontaneous may be weird whether it be sexually, mentally or physically. To your partner, they know you inside and out and when you do something that isn't "you," it may be off-putting.

Oftentimes, you can also meet someone that is not your true love, as stated before. Even so, the relationship can still last longer than you think. Many relationships still function well because it just works.

Partners can be so compatible as a team and work better together than others. They may work better as a team and have a lot of support for one another but may lack a connection in many other categories. They stick together because they both want the relationship to work and they accept each other's flaws as an individual and as a couple.

When couples want to make it work, that increases the longevity of the relationship and that's how you avoid ending your relationship. The moment that either partner doesn't want the relationship to work, it will not. Do things every chance you get to extend the life of your relationship. If you don't, you will be setting your relationship up to fail. By missing the opportunities to secure your relationship's future, as you would anything else in life, you are gearing up to lose that opportunity.

Maybe you should ask yourself if a relationship is what you want. Sometimes, the things we do are a testament to what we truly want. "What was once brand new and exciting has now become routine."

Chemistry Factor #3: Serendipity

"When we only experience one kind of chemistry, we begin to feel like we're not living anymore."

In 1878, Russian chemist Constantin Fahlberg was analyzing the properties of coal tar in Ira Remsen's laboratory at Johns Hopkins University, Baltimore. At the end of a particularly long day, he left the lab to eat dinner. The importance of handwashing had not yet reached mainstream culture, so Fahlberg sat down at the dinner table with his hands covered with chemical residue from his experiments.

He picked up a roll and was surprised to find that it tasted sweet. He returned to his lab and tasted several compounds before he discovered the source of the sweetness. He ascertained that the taste had come from the residue of anhydroorthosulphaminebenzoic acid.

A decade later, Fahlberg patented the product, renaming it saccharine. The product he discovered was 400 times sweeter than natural sugar. Today, we know saccharine as the active ingredient in Sweet'N Low, the artificial sweetener.

Fahlberg's discovery is just one of many accidents of science that have reshaped the world. The microwave oven, Velcro, the pacemaker and LSD were all stumbled upon by scientists seeking to answer questions unrelated to these monumental discoveries. There is some irony in the fact that an accident of fate can have more impact than any carefully calibrated plan of action. This idea holds true when it comes to the chemistry between individuals.

Much of this chapter—and much of this book—serves as a reminder that planning and intention have limits. You might spend hours preparing for a date only to find that there is no spark. Likewise, you might assume that a date is a throwaway, then find yourself overflowing with affection for the other person when you spend more time with them. Years of online dating can result in nothing but frustration while a chance encounter at a bar could change your life forever.

Accidents, whether they are fortunate, unfortunate or neutral, happen every single day. You can spend hours regretting when something doesn't go your way, but the truth is, life has no "undo" or "redo" button. It can often be healthy—even necessary—to draw some lesson from such an event. Humans are hardwired to try and make meaning out of the unexplained.

However, you should avoid spending too much time blaming yourself for what was not entirely in your control. Acknowledge your mistakes, do what you can to improve yourself and keep focused on the present. Many people find it satisfying to punish themselves when a relationship goes bad, but when the punishment removes all the joy and hope from life, you have gone too far.

Even bad relationships leave you with a lesson to learn whether it be good or bad. Perhaps there are a handful of truly evil people out there, but most of us deserve to move through life with a sense of hope.

You may have limited control over whether you experience that spark of chemistry when you meet a new person, but you can be thoughtful and intentional about how to move forward. Some people advocate total transparency and honesty while others prefer to play their cards close to the vest.

When it comes to sharing your initial feelings of attraction, be proactive, not reactive. Try to be certain that you are really feeling what you think you are feeling. Sometimes you can be influenced by the feelings of the other person. For example, after a first date, you might be feeling ambivalent, but the other person requests a second date, so you oblige. When you arrive, you see how full of joy and excitement they are. Emotions are catching. You may find yourself resonating with their feelings when just a few minutes earlier you were feeling apprehensive.

Emotions are the brain's rational responses to stimuli, but that doesn't always mean we can make sense of them. If a person asks you how you feel about them, it is OK to say that you aren't sure or that you aren't ready to talk about emotions yet. They evolve quickly, especially when you are just getting to know someone new.

To put a positive spin on things, meeting a new person is almost always full of surprises. Approach each new interaction by embracing the unknown. There is simply no telling what chemistry will be sparked by a new presence in your life.

Chemistry vs. True Love?

"When you know someone isn't right for you, it's best to pack up your emotions and run."

Context, personality and serendipity are largely responsible for establishing the initial spark of chemistry between two people, but what happens after that spark fades? How does chemistry change over time and how much control do we really have over that evolution?

The chemistry factor will end relationships, but the exception to the rule of chemistry is being with someone who brings out many different kinds of chemistry within you.

We can think of these individuals as our true loves and yes, there a many of them. There isn't just one. It is impossible to have one true love because we are always changing. Who is right for you at this stage in your life will not be right for you when you become a different version of yourself?

We have it in our minds that whoever we settle down with is our true love. But at different times in your life, there are different people who are perfect for you. Your true love is also relevant to the time you're in, in your life, "when you are." We'll get into why there is more than one true love for you in the next chapter.

The exception to the factor of chemistry are the people who accentuate many different types of chemistry within you. Your happiness, the calmness, the joy, the silliness, the love and so much more. They bring out the better sides of you. These types of people are the exception because they are compatible with you. You don't have to try to be happy or comfortable with them; you simply just are. This kind of relationship can easily last a lifetime if both partners want it to. If all opportunities of increasing the longevity and health of the relationship are met, then there will only be small minor issues that can easily be worked through.

There are the exceptions, your true loves, and the people you are compatible with, but the flip side is the people who bring out the worst in you. Have you ever dated someone that you knew wasn't right for you but you stuck with them despite knowing the bad outweighed the good in the relationship? What did it cost you and was it worth it?

In hindsight, we all have 20/20 vision, but it's best to try to make the best decisions in the present rather than lose yourself in an avoidable situation. We all can learn and grow from every situation we've experienced. "When you know someone isn't right for you, it's best to pack up your emotions and run." They will not be worth the pain.

You'll know over the course of your relationship if a person brings out the worst in you because the bad outweighs the good! When you experience that, it is time to leave that relationship, no matter who you're with.

You both may argue a lot for what, in retrospect, always seems to be because of a silly reason and over something small. That's the result of having no tolerance for each other along with a lack of respect and compassion. You both are over the relationship, but neither of you will just let it die.

Naturally, when we are holding onto our relationship but we know it should end, we are thinking of the way things once were, what we knew was possible and how we felt when it was good despite how short that goodness lasts as it comes and goes. We like to think things will get better. Even when we know they never well, we still stay in that relationship with a handful of hope and, at times, no self-love left, all just to please the other person.

The love for ourselves has been shifted into a trained mentality to stick through the rough situation and hopefully see the light at the end of the tunnel someday.

Even though all relationships inevitably end, that does not mean you can't have a beautiful relationship with compassion and respect for one another. You don't have to be in a tunnel or a dark place if you don't want to. End that toxic relationship immediately. If the person is crazy, take a discrete route to safely distance yourself. Get a restraining order if you have to.

"Hope is great when you feel like you have no control, but at some point, you have to take control." You stay in the relationship because you're holding onto the things that you really like about the relationship. This is very unhealthy, especially with what is being thrown at you every day while you hold onto what little good remains.

If you stick around long enough, you become stuck and lose yourself without even realizing it. Even when your friends and family tell you, you might see it, yet the hope that the person will change remains as you focus on the light at the end of the tunnel without realizing it because you're so desperate for your partner to change.

Your focus will be on staying with that person vs. having a great experience while you're with them. This happens because your hope is in them to change and not your ability to do so for yourself. You can't even depend on yourself for help anymore. "It's more draining to give yourself a try so instead, you give yourself away."

"It's hard to tell what you're capable of when you surrender your will to someone else." You become a subject to their rule. It's always better to choose yourself over anyone, especially when they continuously prove to be against you and push you away. "They are choosing themselves and you are choosing them as well, so who is left to choose you?"

Chemistry: After the Honeymoon

"If you don't have respect for yourself, then who will?"

As mentioned earlier in this book:
- Some people bring out your adventurous side.
- Some people bring out your silliness.

- Some people bring out a better version of you.
- Some people will disappoint you.
- Some people will bore you.
- Some people will abuse you.
- Some people make life worth living.

This list of statements might read like a poem or even song lyrics. If you listen closely to popular music in this decade or those past, you will notice a pattern. Artists are always singing about love. Finding love. Losing love. Wondering about the nature of love. Missing love. Needing love. The love song can really be considered a genre, one that spans all musical styles from folk to country, R&B, hip hop and beyond.

One of the reasons for this may be the fact that the word "love" still has no widely accepted definition. The Oxford English Dictionary has several definitions for love, and none really captures the *feeling* of being in love:

- Love (noun) – An intense feeling of deep affection
- Love (noun) – A great interest and pleasure in something

Historically, love has been closely associated with commitment. When you love someone, you are dedicated to them. You make sacrifices for them. You may be preoccupied with their well-being and make changes that put the object of your love close to the center of your life.

Society itself is oriented towards this type of commitment. The institution of marriage is the legal—and often religious—structure that legitimizes and rewards the union of two individuals. Societies incentivize marriage by offering tax breaks and other benefits to those who choose to enter marriage under the law.

This is the reality because most people believe that such unions benefit children and society as a whole. A great deal of research seems to confirm this. Married couples are generally happier than single people (though there is a caveat to this, which will be explained later), and children raised with two parents in the home have a greater chance at succeeding by many measures.

However, in modern society, love and commitment no longer always go hand in hand. An increasing percentage of people choose to delay marriage or engage in non-marital cohabitation. Therefore, the connection between love and commitment is sometimes difficult to observe.

In many parts of the world, arranged marriages are commonplace. You can easily observe how love is not at all a requirement for marriage. In fact, a 2016 study from the University of Lincoln, United Kingdom, indicates that those in arranged marriages may be happier in the long run. Researchers attribute this to the phenomenon of unrealistic expectations. If your bar for love is set lower, you are less likely to be disappointed.

So, it is, of course, possible to love someone and not want to marry them. Likewise, two people can get married and not love each other. Love is just one of those things that cannot easily be observed or measured. It is no wonder that artists spend so much time and effort writing and singing about it.

In most Western cultures, including America, about 90% of people will marry at least once by the age of 50. Almost half of these marriages end in divorce (after reaching this point in the book, you know how the other half of marriages will end). The likelihood of divorce increases for those who marry more than once.

How does this all relate to chemistry?

At the outset of this chapter, we made a distinction between the chemistry that sparks romance and the chemistry that sustains it over the long term. Love plays an important role in how this chemistry develops. It is also an element of chemistry that you actually have some control over.

It is an unfair fact of the world that some people are just much luckier than the rest of us. Some experience that initial spark of chemistry. They feel physical lust for each other and quickly form a deep emotional and psychological bond. This often is the result of a shared context and common interests.

When the initial spark fades, some lucky couples easily transition into their long-term kind of chemistry. Conflicts rarely arise and they can easily diffuse them when they do. They share goals for the future and a similar or complementary approach to life. As they age, they continue to delight in each other's company. They still surprise each other and remain generous with their time and affection. They live a comfortable life that shields them from the kinds of hardships that strain relationships to the breaking point. They fall in love and they stay that way until one partner passes away.

Unfortunately, only a very, very small percentage of relationships are like this. The sheer amount of good fortune necessary for such a relationship is just not something most people can come by in a lifetime. We might call these individuals "soul mates." We might say that each has found "the one," their one "true love." Entertainment and media reinforce the idea that everyone can have this kind of relationship. We all grow up thinking that we have a shot at that fairy-tale ending. The fact is, for most of us, this reality is out of reach.

However, there is no reason to be sad or frustrated by this truth.

When you begin a new relationship, you cannot just continue hoping for that fairy tale to come true. When two people make an emotional investment in one another, they need to be proactive in keeping the relationship healthy and on the right course.

After the honeymoon period ends, you may need to adjust the relationship dynamic. You may have to make an effort compared to when things were natural and easy. This is not a sign that your relationship is failing. It is a sign that you need to make a decision: Invest more into the relationship or watch it slowly die by a lack of effort to make it grow.

Human psychology compels most people towards comfort. We want our daily lives to be as easy and stress-free as possible. For this reason, a comfortable relationship can begin to feel stale or boring. You may no longer feel like you and your partner are "living life." It may begin to feel like life is passing you by and that all you have is your routine. You may feel inclined to blame your partner while dodging all responsibility for the state of things. Needless to say, placing blame, especially without any self-reflection, is toxic chemistry. In this way, chemistry has the power to end relationships, not just to start them.

Your actions and behaviors, at least when they concern your partner, can alter the chemistry of your relationship. Over time, it can become something you hardly recognize.

There is a deep kind of tragedy to what we might call "falling out of love." It is the kind of pain that people write novels and poems about. It is not something anyone wants to experience, at least in the midst of it.

The hope is that by taking a thoughtful approach to meeting people and paying close attention to first impressions, you can give yourself a better chance of finding a partner who will work with you to keep the relationship moving in the best direction. If you find that you are the only one putting forth any effort, you should consider this a serious red flag.

If you've ever been in a long-term relationship, you understand that it is possible to hold two contrasting ideas simultaneously. On the one hand, you want more spontaneity in your life. You may feel stifled, even trapped, by your partner and the routine that is your daily life. At the same time, you may fear a loss of that stability. You are resistant to making a change because you don't want to hurt or upset your partner without good reason. If you've been together for years, you may strongly resist the idea of throwing it all away and starting over.

The condition of holding two or more contrasting ideas in your head at one time is called *cognitive dissonance*. Rest assured, it is something that everyone deals with in life. In reality, we experience it quite often.

You know you need to lose weight, yet you desire another helping of dessert. You know you need to save money, yet you feel pressure to purchase new clothes. The same idea holds true for relationships. They are far more complicated than food or clothes. Fortunately, when dealing with cognitive dissonance in a relationship, you don't have to deal with it alone. Your partner can help you figure out what to do.

However, before you broach the subject with your significant other, be sure that you have thought carefully about the situation. Here are some questions to ask yourself. Thinking about these questions is good, but writing your answers down is even better. When you write, you tap into other parts of your brain. It helps you see connections and patterns that you might otherwise miss.

- Is your discomfort new or has it been building for a while? For how long?
- Can you point to specific situations, conversations or actions that have caused you to feel this way? Or is your cognitive dissonance more abstract and diffuse?
- When was the last time that you experienced joy or delight with your partner? How many of these moments can you remember from the past three months?
- If your relationship ended tomorrow, what might your life be like three months from now?

Writing down your answers will provide you with a starting point to what could end up being a difficult conversation with your partner. Hopefully, they will appreciate the effort you went through. Your writing can act as a kind of "evidence" that you are engaging with your partner in good faith. It is a different way of investing in your relationship and the benefits could be immense.

The Conclusion of Chemistry

"When there just isn't enough chemistry."

Don't let this section heading depress you. As we have seen, endings are just another phase of the human experience. All relationships inevitably end. Society and culture have produced so many euphemisms to describe how and why relationships end. You've probably heard friends and family utter at least one of the following phrases. Perhaps you've used them yourself:

- *We grew apart.*
- *It just wasn't working.*
- *Our priorities changed.*
- *We weren't happy.*
- *I felt trapped.*
- *Things got too hard.*
- *We wanted different things.*
- *I needed a change.*
- *We lost our spark.*
- *The thrill was gone.*

The most remarkable thing about these phrases is how vague they are. How sad that we can only offer platitudes after something that we have invested so much in. Ask yourself why so many of us use such trite language to describe breakups when the person we are no longer together with used to mean the world to us.

Unfortunately, relationships hardly ever end at the right time. To make substantial changes in life, humans often need to be pushed past the breaking point. This is when behaviors like cheating, lying, arguing and even physical violence can manifest.[1]

Research data based on surveys indicate that as many as 10 million people suffer some form of domestic abuse each year in the United States. Barely 10% get reported to authorities. Individuals are complicated and some suffer from mental health issues that may cause them to lash out at the ones they love. However, you have no responsibility to stay in an abusive relationship, no matter how much you love or sympathize with your abuser. If you have abused someone, the safest thing to do is isolate yourself and seek counseling or mental health counseling.

So, how does chemistry relate to the end of a relationship?

The chemistry you share with your partner can change over time. It can also be altered by major life events outside of the relationship, such as a death in your immediate circle, a new job or a new living arrangement. It is rare for chemistry to just change on its own unless a great deal of time has elapsed. Relationships are not closed systems; they are constantly bombarded by external stimuli. Life exerts pressure on the bonds that hold people together, just like it puts pressure on the people themselves. Counseling or therapy can alter the chemistry of a relationship as well whether it's in a good or bad way.

If you no longer find delight in the chemistry you share with your partner, there are concrete actions you can take.

---

[1] *No one—no one!—deserves to be abused, either physically, psychologically, or emotionally. If you live in the United States, and you are living with abuse or the fear of abuse, contact the National Domestic Violence Hotline. 1-800-799-SAFE or visit www.thehotline.org. If you are in imminent physical danger, call 911. Try and get to a safe place—in public with lots of people around.

Most of them relate to growth and experience, which we will address in the next two chapters. For now, here are the basics.

New experiences

Share novel experiences with your partner. Get outside your comfort zone. Put yourself in the position to show your partner a different side of yourself.

Therapy or counseling

If you or your partner has fallen into a damaging pattern of behavior, change can be extremely difficult without outside help. Many people will feel safer speaking their minds in therapy and this can be incredibly freeing. Sometimes, the kindest thing you can do for your partner is to bring in a neutral third party to help work things out. Therapy is a good start to changing a rough time in the relationship. This book will share a valuable practice to help you through a rough time in the chapter titled "Therapy."

Take a break

When done properly and kindly, time apart can recharge you and provide a much-needed perspective. The break doesn't need to be long! A weekend, or even just an evening apart, can remind you why you got together with your partner in the first place. As mentioned before, when done properly and with good and kind intentions, a break will be all your relationship needed to get back on track in the right direction. Some people today use a break as a way to be single for a brief moment in their relationship and date or have sex with someone else. That type of break will not help your relationship.

Find your own community

Having your own group of acquaintances or friends is extremely important for the long-term health of a relationship. You need to be able to vent! It is OK to "complain" about the little things that your partner does that you find annoying or frustrating. If, however, you find yourself only talking about the negatives, consider this a red flag. Do some thinking or writing about why it is so hard to speak lovingly about your significant other.

We'll go more in-depth and add to this list in future chapters. For now, let's assume that you have tried at least two of these strategies and given them some time to work—at least three months. Psychologists generally agree that it takes around 21 days to establish a new habit and as many as 66 days for that habit to become automatic. Change doesn't happen overnight. If you make a change and still don't see a difference in your relationship chemistry, give it time before making a more drastic shift.

It is often easier, especially in a new relationship, to give up before really investing in yourself and your partner. But if you've really put in the effort and still aren't happy, it may be time to call it quits. When it comes to long-term relationships, frustration and boredom can be overpowering. There will be a deeper discussion of the dynamics of a breakup in future chapters, but for now, let's take a look at what you might expect after it happens—in terms of chemistry.

Many relationships don't end with one partner saying that it's time to call it quits. Most people choose to act as a way of signaling the desire to break up. Cheating and lying are the two most common actions in this situation. They are really a form of relationship sabotage. Ironically, it can feel easier than just saying what is on your mind.

Either way, you will be faced with a choice: to keep your ex in your life or not. Hopefully, your ex won't try to insert themselves into your life after the relationship is over. Situations like this can range from annoying to dangerous. If you are fearful that your partner will continue contacting you against your wishes, you can seek help. Such behavior can evolve into stalking, which is a punishable offense.

Barring such a situation, the choice is yours. Some people end up becoming friends with their ex, and this new relationship will have a different kind of chemistry. Sure, you two may get along great but in most cases, the relationship ended for a reason. You've been through a lot with this person. They may know a side of you that you haven't shown to other people. There is no shame in keeping such a person in your life, unless, of course, they are preventing you from moving on or growing.

To some degree, the most important thing to understand about relationship chemistry is that you don't have full control over it. Subsequent chapters will focus on elements of relationships that can be more easily altered.

Obligation vs. Inspiration

"Find joy in who your partner is, not who you want them to be."

How much power an individual has over the chemistry of their relationship is debatable. Humans have very few tools to combat the effects of time and biology.

Sometimes, people approach relationships like they would a fixer-upper house. A house may need a lot of work, but you buy it because you envision what it *could be*. You know there are concrete steps to take to make the dream a reality. You know the house will need some renovations, a new coat of paint, maybe a new roof or remodeled kitchen. On top of this, you have a general idea of how much it will cost to get from point A to B. In short, a fixer-upper is inspiring. It fills you with hope and ideas that you are excited to bring to fruition.

You can experience similar feelings at the outset of a new relationship. You may be inspired by visions of a beautiful future with your new spouse. This sense of hope is a beautiful thing and it is responsible for the bump of happiness you feel when meeting the "right" person. However, this hope, like all things, will not remain unchanged by time and circumstances.

Instead of focusing solely on your partner as the source of your inspiration, focus on the relationship itself as well. Find inspiration in the things you will do together. The home and family you may build, the experiences you might share and the growth that you will both create for one another. Find joy in who your partner is, not who you want them to be.

This doesn't mean you cannot play a role in your partner's growth. You might encourage them to try new things and get outside their comfort zone. You might invest time and resources in them, but don't do it because you expect something in return. Do it because you want to see them flourish. If you expect something in return or have a predetermined outcome, you will be disappointed when your partner does not meet the result you desired.

A common shift in relationship chemistry is inspiration to obligation. This can typically occur after 6 months to a year or so of being together. Rather than caring because you want to, you find yourself caring because you have to. This obligation leads to the feeling of being trapped. Some people experience feeling trapped throughout the course of their relationship mainly dependent on chemistry. This feeling need not last. Subsequent chapters illustrate and describe many ways to end the cycle of obligation and reclaim the sense of inspiration that you experienced when your relationship was still new.

Representatives

"If the other person doesn't like who you really are, then you should find out as soon as possible."

Since the first date is your first opportunity to assess the chemistry you have with a potential partner, it is useful to consider how individuals tend to approach such meetings. Consciously or not, people put forth great effort to make a good first impression. As mentioned earlier in this chapter, first impressions can be difficult to alter. When the stakes are high, there is an incentive for individuals to hide the negative parts of themselves and exaggerate the positives.

It may be helpful to think of a first date as a meeting of ambassadors or representatives. In diplomacy, an ambassador represents the interests of their country. They must project strength, competency and a willingness to negotiate in good faith.

A first date is not so different. Keep in mind that your potential partner has a strong incentive to make a good impression. If you choose to get to know them better, don't be surprised if you see a side that you don't like as much. Rather than react with anger or betrayal, consider how you can be compassionate and understanding. After all, you likely did the same thing on that first date.

There is a difference between sending your best "representative" to a first date and telling outright lies. Lying or concealing important information actually says more about your character than the truth would. A person whose first instinct is to tell lies about themselves may not be a person who is ready for a trusting relationship. Some information should never be concealed. For example, if you have a sexually transmissible disease, you must tell your potential partner before you have sex. There is nothing wrong with wanting to avoid difficult topics on a first date. Just don't lie if you are confronted about them.

The best strategy is to represent yourself honestly on a first date. If the other person doesn't like who you really are, then you should find that out as soon as possible. No matter how attractive and successful a person is, you will not have a fulfilling relationship if either of you misrepresent yourselves.

Sexual compatibility is discussed more extensively in other sections, but it is useful to mention a few things here. It is much harder for a person to hide their sexuality than it is to hide their personality. Some people prefer to wait a while after meeting someone new while others see an advantage in checking their compatibility sooner rather than later. Both approaches have advantages and disadvantages. It is up to the person to decide when they are ready for sex or physical intimacy.

Whenever you decide to get to know a potential partner in that way, keep a few ideas in mind.

Desire is difficult to hide. If someone expresses a particular desire during sex, it is most likely genuine. However, the first time that a couple has sex, it is not necessarily an indication of what sex will be like in the future.

Many studies have shown that sex tends to become more satisfying as a couple gets to know one another. When two people feel safe together, they may be more willing to reveal desires that they keep hidden. Of course, as time passes, things can get stale if neither partner makes an effort to switch things up within the range of what they're naturally interested in and willing to do. Trying something completely new to please your partner can backfire and turn them off if they know that isn't what you're into.

Sexual chemistry is necessary for many couples, but not all. Even if you aren't ready to have sex with your new partner, talk about how you view sex in the context of a relationship. How important is it really to you? You can even discuss how often you hope to have sex. Such questions can help you ascertain compatibility when the stakes are lower.

Growth

"Who is right for you now will not be right for you forever because you are continuously growing and becoming a different version of yourself."

The 1989 Rob Reiner film, *When Harry Met Sally*, has become the archetypal romantic comedy. It set the groundwork for numerous subsequent films of this genre, including *Sleepless in Seattle, Clueless, Love, Actually, 50 First Dates, The Best Man, You've Got Mail, The Wedding Singer, Forgetting Sarah Marshall, Boomerang, There's Something About Mary, Serendipity, How Stella Got Her Groove Back* and countless others. These films are funny for the same reason they are heartwarming; they all highlight the unpredictable nature of love between two people. They remind us that an enduring relationship takes much more than just "meeting the right person."

Spoiler alert starts here! Scroll past the next five paragraphs to skip the spoiler!

The script for *When Harry Met Sally* was written by Nora Ephron. It depicts the titular characters during key moments of their 12-year history together. It begins when friends Harry (Billy Crystal) and Sally (Meg Ryan) graduate from the University of Chicago and drive to New York City to begin their careers. After an awkward conversation at a diner, they part ways on unfriendly terms. Five years later, they meet again on a flight. Harry is engaged and Sally is in a serious relationship. Their conversation reminds them how much they enjoyed each other's company, but they agree that building a friendship at this point in their lives would be a bad idea.

Fast-forward another six years when the two share another chance encounter at a bookstore. Harry reports that his wife left him for another man and Sally's relationship has also imploded. They bond over their "failed" relationships, eventually settling into an easy friendship. They share many late-night phone conversations about their experiences with love and disappointment.

At a New Year's Eve party, Harry and Sally finally acknowledge their mutual attraction, but given their history, they each decide that a romantic relationship is out of the question. Soon after, Sally's ex-husband gets engaged and she becomes deeply depressed. Harry attempts to comfort her and they end up having sex for the first time. After a heated argument, they part ways yet again.

Another year goes by. On New Year's Eve, Harry declares his love for Sally, but she thinks that he is only saying he loves her out of loneliness. However, after recounting their long and turbulent history, they decide to get married 12 years and three months after that fateful road trip to New York City.

The story of *When Harry Met Sally* is beloved in part because of its happy ending. It plays out like a fairy tale: Two friends share over a decade of chance encounters, heartbreak and setbacks only to end up declaring their love for one another and getting married. However, few people know that the movie script's original ending did not end in marriage. Harry and Sally simply parted ways yet again, their fairy-tale ending far from assured.

Spoiler alert ends here!

Perhaps the original ending would have resulted in a less popular and beloved film, but would the story be any less real?

Happily Ever After?

"If you are only seeking out 'the perfect' partner, no one will ever measure up."

The desire for a "perfect fairy-tale relationship" is reinforced in many of us from a very young age. Disney films, popular with adults and children alike, are replete with quests for "true love." On a rational level, you probably understand that such a relationship is rare, but how many of your decisions are made with this very idea in mind?

Humans are hardwired to seek confirmation bias; we thrive on information that confirms what we already believe. By the same token, we often tune out or discount information that contradicts our beliefs. If you have made up your mind that your current partner is your "true love," then you are more likely to overlook their flaws.

This can be a good thing—after all, no one is perfect—but it can also make you blind to red flags or other warning signs that indicate there may be trouble on the horizon. One of the most challenging tasks for a couple is to view the flaws in their relationship from the proper perspective. If you are only seeking out "the perfect" partner, then no one will ever measure up. Likewise, if you've made up your mind that your relationship *will be* perfect, then you may let many kind, loyal and supportive people walk out the door.

When Harry Met Sally reminds us that what works in the present may not work in the future. It also highlights the truth that what works for your present self might not have worked when you were younger. As time passes, you inevitably grow in response to changes in your circumstances. Your priorities change. Your needs change. It stands to reason that what you need in a partner will change as well.

The goal of this book is not to help you find your "happily ever after." In a way, your "happily ever after" can arrive at any time with or without a partner. "Happily ever after," for our purposes, means accepting your circumstances as they are. It means that you will be happy with your partner, by yourself or circumstance because it is what you want and not what you're settling for. It means finding joy and satisfaction in the present moment, even when things are far from perfect. It means having an attitude of gratitude for what you have and carrying a realistic sense of hope for the future.

If you are currently in a relationship, "happily ever after" means honoring your partner and the commitment you share. It means approaching all conflicts with a sense of open-minded goodwill. "Happily ever after" also means knowing when a relationship is at its end while minimizing the emotional and psychological damage suffered by yourself and your partner.

Ongoing Opportunities

"Be present in your relationship or you will not have one."

Bamboo is one of the fastest-growing plants. Some species can grow several inches in just an afternoon. The bamboo that is knee-high in the morning could be as tall as the average male adult by midnight. You can sit there and actually *see* the growth happen. Unfortunately, people do not grow like bamboo and neither do relationships.

After our adolescent years, our bodies cease to grow. Of course, we still change through the process of aging. Physical growth, however, is not what is at issue here. When it comes to relationships, we are concerned with emotional and psychological growth. Committing to a relationship means committing to a process of shared growth. Without this commitment, most relationships will not be able to endure hardships.

When you meet a person, you have no idea of their growth trajectory. This is why people usually don't get married after just one date. It takes time to get to know a person and form some idea of how they envision their future. All plans are subject to change, but knowing the inner motivations of your partner—or potential partner—can go a long way in helping you form a picture of what they might be like one, five or even 10 years down the road.

Growth is inevitable. For our purposes, we'll define growth as the process of developing and maturing with time. You probably know someone who never seems to grow. They are stuck in a period of arrested development or immaturity. We will take it as a given that these individuals, too, are growing and developing. They just may be developing in a way that makes it more difficult for them to achieve success or stability. Since everyone grows unpredictably and at their own rate, you can see how growth can be a major factor in determining the outcome of a relationship.

We are always chasing the perfect fairy-tale relationship. If no one is perfect, how can we possibly find a perfect relationship? I'll tell you! We can't because a perfect relationship does not exist.

Sure, your relationship can be great and issue-free. But even in that issue-free relationship, some things are unsaid most times to continue to keep it perfect. If neither of you are mentioning any issues, then there probably isn't one, right? Or, maybe your relationship is still in the honeymoon phase. If you checked "no" for all of those, then maybe you truly do have the perfect relationship. That relationship is perfect for you—for now.

Growth is another main factor that will end a relationship no matter how compatible you and your partner are. As stated in the "Chemistry" chapter, we are all continuously growing. Who is perfect for you now will not be perfect for you in the future. When you think of your past experiences, some of them seem like a lifetime ago to the point that you were once a completely different person. You've grown so much. Memories and nostalgia are the remnants of what once was.

All relationships inevitably end. Who is right for you now will not be right for you forever because we are continuously growing and becoming a different version of ourselves.

We've been taught that when we get married, we will have a "happily ever after." That's not the case. When you get married or get into a relationship, the countdown begins because it is the beginning of the end.

When you meet someone, there are so many things that must go right for the relationship to work. Granted, in the beginning, you both make it happen, especially because it is so new and the interest is beyond high. After some time being together, one or both of you will grow. You can grow together or one can grow without the other. That doesn't necessarily mean that the one growing is better than the other in any way and lastly, you both can grow in different directions because you both are growing apart.

When growth is happening in a relationship, it symbolizes the end; unless both partners are growing together or are both understanding of each other and want to grow together. The length of a relationship can be extended countless amounts of times only if you both continue to value each other's love, trust, honesty and loyalty.

If you both are always communicating and looking at the relationship objectively to see what is truly wrong with it, you will stay together and your unity and bond will grow deeper and stronger every time. This will be discussed further in the "Therapy" chapter.

As you grow together, you're still learning about each other. You did it together because you both wanted to stay together and make the relationship work. The chances of this are low because it is also hard to want to grow in the same direction and at the same time.

Before and after you were a couple, you were an individual first. Your wants and desires will most likely be different from your partner's. So, the direction you grow will be different as well.

Sometimes a partner growing while the other stays the same may bring about a growth and support system. If your relationship experiences a support system, your partnership will be tested due to the shift of power while one partner is forced to show more support. It will be difficult if that partner isn't used to that role. The chances of your relationship surviving are also low because of the ups and downs your relationship will go through. Even before the main factors run their course, your relationship will be continuously tested from day one.

In a relationship, individual growth continues along with the growth of the relationship. Most partners constantly focus on the relationship which seems like the right thing to do, but it is not entirely correct. That is only one part of it.

Relationship growth is important, but unless you also focus on personal growth, you will not be able to understand issues if they arise from an individual level. The relationship, as a unit, cannot trump everything.

When there are individual growth problems, your significant other may think of it as your problem and that you need to handle it rather than thinking of your issues as their own. That becomes an obstacle to strengthening the foundation of the overall relationship as a whole. When this happens, the relationship will end because the person with the issue will feel neglected over time or they'll stop confiding in their partner. That will impact the relationship negatively and ultimately end it just because they didn't trust each other enough to feel comfortable communicating their feelings. They weren't confident enough to talk to their spouse without being judged.

Growth and change are inevitable whether you're single or in a relationship. As we grow, our wants, desires, values, beliefs and interests change due to our experiences. If partners are not growing at the same rate or direction, they will grow apart which will ultimately end the relationship. We are continuously experiencing life as we grow and becoming a different version of ourselves while fundamentally staying the same.

Growth in time determines who is right for you today, tomorrow and yesterday. Time is always passing and we are always growing so no one is right for you forever!

Some people may say, "I'm right about the person that I ended up with. They are my true love," but there are many people that are married and a true love is unfortunately not what they ended up with. Even if you picked the perfect person for you today, there is no guarantee that they will be right for you later in the relationship.

People continue to grow one day at a time so just hope you're willing to adapt to the growth and change when they come. Many divorces happen each year. The divorce rate has been declining year after year but not because more couples are staying together. It's because along with the divorce rate declining, so is the marriage rate.

More people are questioning the idea of marriage. Other than it being such a financial endeavor, religion and the religious basis for marriage is being questioned as well. The less people that believe in religion, the less people believe in a traditional marriage. They used to go hand in hand with each other. Now people get married without God as a witness. They may even have a marriage in their own way.

So many people cheat and marriages seem to always have issues that ultimately lead to divorce. Many people might have been the perfect person for each other when they married, but over time that will always change.

Again, every relationship has the potential for its life to be extended. If you both want the relationship to work, it can last many years to come but only if you both do what is necessary to be happy as a couple and for yourselves while in the relationship.

When it's time to decide to get into a relationship, many truly believe that they are in love and have met the right person. What ends up happening is, yes, they met the right person, but the major factors ran their course. Chemistry, growth and experience played a factor that brought about the end of those relationships.

The main factors will always end a relationship. The person who is right for you now is mainly based on time and "when you are." "When you are" is about where you are in terms of the timeline of your life and your growth. At that moment, both partners are ready for each other. It's always a beautiful moment because it's based on their true feelings, that two people met each other and that they decided to be together. Everything in that moment from the timing to the mutual care for each other is perfect. But, it is only going to last if the desire for each other is still there with the goal to stay together and make the relationship work.

To confront the effects of individual growth, a relationship requires honesty, loyalty and trust.

Trust

In a relationship lacking trust, one partner may be afraid to grow. They may fear that their partner will not like the new version of them. Any relationship that hampers the growth of one or both partners is not built on a solid foundation.

Without trust, suspicion and resentment can run rampant causing all manner of tension and conflict.

A trusting relationship, by contrast, is one where each partner knows that the other has their best interest in mind. They will celebrate one another's growth without letting jealousy or resentment take hold. A trusting relationship can still end due to the effects of growth, but it will likely be a more amicable way and mature split.

Loyalty

When one partner experiences growth in a relationship that lacks loyalty, toxic behaviors can ensue. Resentment can take hold and lead to cheating or other forms of betrayal. The growing partner may be overcome with guilt and made to suffer for their hard work and success. Such behaviors initiate a cycle of resentment that will continue until all the goodwill of the relationship is eaten away.

In a relationship built on loyalty, each partner will remind the other that they would never stand in the way of positive growth. A loyal relationship that ends because of growth can be very tragic.

It is hard to imagine a loyal relationship ever coming to an end, let alone for an inevitable factor like growth. Still, you can remain loyal to your partner even during a breakup. You may no longer feel loyalty for the relationship itself, but you can remain loyal to your partner by looking out for their well-being even when it hurts. In most cases, there is usually one partner who remains loyal while the other is selfish and focused on self.

Honesty

Honesty is one of the ways that trust is built. Partners must be truthful with one another even when it is difficult. In a way, honesty is most important at the start of a relationship; it can set the groundwork for all future communication. Would you rather be in a relationship where you always trust your partner's words or one where your partner only tells you what they think you want to hear?

Honesty can be hard, especially when it comes to sensitive issues like a person's appearance or aspects of their personality that are beyond their control. If your partner has short legs, is it really beneficial to express your distaste or criticism? Honesty isn't helpful when there is really nothing the other person can do about it.

Honesty, in the wrong context, can be cruel. However, if your partner asks for your honest opinion, you should not mince words. You might also consider telling your partner other truths. They may have short legs, but you love them anyway. If you don't love them, then this conversation may lead to something deeper that needs to be addressed.

The healthiest way to view growth is as an inevitable phenomenon. There is simply no guarantee that the person you meet—or fall in love with—is the person who will be looking back at you from across the dinner table three or four years from now. Likewise, there is a great likelihood that you, too, will change.

You might not be able to see growth when it happens. For this reason, it is important to self-reflect every once in a while. Every month or so, take some time for yourself and think or write about how things have changed over the previous four weeks. The insights you glean can be used to strengthen your relationship. It might also indicate the presence of a deeper issue that warrants a conversation.

Individual Growth vs. Relationship Growth

"If you want to extend the life of your relationship, you must always make choices that are good for you and your partner."

In a relationship, individual growth continues to happen along with the growth of the relationship. For many people, it seems natural to focus more on the relationship than on their individual development.

As mentioned earlier, individual growth is important to the longevity of relationships. When you love someone, you want your life together to be great. However, neglecting your individual development does your partner no favors. Relationship growth is important, but without also focusing on individual growth, many potential pitfalls could be missed.

Ironically, your partner may be more attuned to your own growth than you are. They may notice small changes over time that you are missing because you are so focused on the relationship. They can also notice the things you should change to become your best self. Usually what they notice is biased towards how they want you to be, but if you agree with the changes they propose and you know it's for a better you, then embrace it no matter how stubborn you may be.

It is important to focus on your own development so that you can share your thoughts with your partner. More likely than not, *they want to be part of your development.* One of the most satisfying elements of a healthy relationship is the knowledge that you make your partner better. Years later, you can look back and feel proud of the way you helped each other. Maybe you encouraged your partner to apply for a job or go back to school. Hopefully, they will also be grateful for the proactive way you helped them grow. Never lose sight of the fact that a relationship consists of individuals with their own unique needs, goals and desires.

Growth cannot happen in an instant. It requires the passage of time. In the "Chemistry" chapter, we discussed how relationship chemistry changes as time goes by. The connection between growth and chemistry is clear: As you grow, your chemistry with your partner changes. When this happens—as it inevitably will—your reaction will determine the course of the relationship. You might have met the right person, but over time this can change. Accepting this possibility is a vital part of establishing a healthy relationship. This acceptance can help you extend the life of a relationship and navigate the various conflicts that arise. Accept the truth and you can make it work.

Relationship Stages

"Love is real and hopefully everyone gets to experience it."

We all want to connect with someone. Whether it's for a short time or forever, it's still a beautiful thing to experience.

A relationship develops rapidly at the outset. As the years go by, development and growth become less predictable. You may go through months, or even years, when things just feel like they aren't changing. If both partners are happy, we might call this a period of stability. If things are less ideal, "stagnant" may be a better descriptor. Everyone wants a stable relationship, but no one wants one that feels stagnant or stuck.

The unpredictable nature of relationship growth makes it difficult to pinpoint when growth poses the most significant threat to relationship stability. However, there are a few key events and occasions that might be used as opportunities to check in with your partner and reassess.

#1 – The first six months

For any relationship that lasts beyond a few dates, the first six months are crucial. At first, each partner experiences a sense of curiosity about their new partner. Hopefully, they ask a lot of questions and have the opportunity to engage with different parts of their new partner's life: their friends, family, hobbies and work-life. If you've ever been at this stage of a relationship, you know how wonderful it feels.

There is a danger hidden here. When things are going well, you may not be inclined to "rock the boat" by asking questions or revealing something about yourself that you think your partner may not like. For this reason, it may take six months or longer before you really learn who your partner is at a deep level. These kinds of revelations can bring you closer, but they can also bring the relationship closer to its end.

The six-month mark offers a signpost that should prompt you to check in with your partner. Consider asking these questions:

- In what ways is our relationship working for you?
- In what ways might it work better?

- How often do you think about the future of this relationship?
- Do you anticipate any major life changes in the next year or so?

While it may seem dorky or even rude to ask these questions, you should feel free enough to ask them or your own version of them. If your partner doesn't want to answer, that is, of course, their right, and you need not hold it against them. However, if they consistently refuse to engage with you on meaningful issues related to the relationship, you might consider this a red flag.

Relationship growth can happen rapidly in the first six months when two people are getting to know each other. If you don't see much growth, ask yourself why. What is holding you and your partner back from achieving a deeper relationship?

#2 – Moving in together

A 2019 Quartz analysis of the Stanford *How Couples Meet and Stay Together Survey* found that about 25% of couples move in together after four months of dating while 50% move in after a year. After two years, about 70% of couples have moved in together, and by the four-year mark, that number reaches 90%. Hopefully, a great deal of growth has occurred before this major life event. Even so, you can expect a rapid amount of growth in the first six months of moving in with your partner.

There will be the honeymoon period—one or more months— when you are still setting the place up and making it a home. Hopefully, it hasn't taken a long time to finally live together because if the relationship is withering away, it stands to reason that neither of you has much tolerance for the other and living together would be a nightmare.

If you both are on the same page in the honeymoon phase and are still excited to move in together, then things should go normally. After that phase ends, couples may have a lot of work to do to grow into their new roles as co-habitators. There are questions to ask at this point as well:

- What boundaries would you like to set up now that we live together?
- How do you envision our lives changing now that we live together?
- What are you most excited about?
- What concerns you the most?

There is a time and a place for questions like these. If your partner had a tough day, then maybe save these questions for a time when you are both calm and receptive. It may be ideal to even set up regular check-ins with your partner after a major life shift like moving in together. Set aside 10 minutes or so every week at a time that works for both of you. Keep in mind that if you both want to make it work, you both should be willing to make some concessions.

#3 – After a transgression like cheating or lying

For many people, a cheating spouse is a deal-breaker. However, a conversation can still take place. People are notoriously bad at providing accurate reasons for their actions. Whatever explanations we come up with are generated after the fact. For a lesser offense, like lying about your whereabouts or misleading your partner about something, conversations are even more critical. Some questions to ask at this juncture include:

- Do you want this relationship to work? Why or why not?
- What can we do going forward to prevent this from happening again?
- If our relationship had ended a month ago, what would your life be like right now?

Running a counterfactual like this can help you and your partner better grasp the possible ramifications of a big decision like ending the relationship. A counterfactual is just a possibility. It is kind of like a hypothetical, but you can use the evidence of your life in the period since it happened. Counterfactuals can provide a great deal of perspective and even remind you or your partner why you are together. They can provide a much-needed shot of gratitude in times of strife.

Remember, your actions dictate how much longer the relationship will last. If you care about your partner and the relationship, you will take the steps necessary to make it work. If you notice that your partner is not making the same effort, consider this a red flag.

A quick note about cheating. There is no guarantee that your partner will find out, but there is no guarantee that they won't either. More often than not, cheating will damage a relationship even if your partner doesn't find out. Cheating once and not getting caught only leads to more cheating, more risk-taking and more of a chance that you will get caught. Think about it this way: What is the prize you win for cheating on your spouse? If you want a relationship to end, there are many kinder ways to do it.

Cheating also weakens your bond with your partner. Even if you feel a sense of gratitude for them afterward, that feeling will fade and be replaced by contempt. No matter what stage of the relationship you are in, integrity is absolutely key. Worst of all, when it comes to cheating, one risks catching a sexually transmitted disease or worse that can put your partner in harm's way.

#4 – Making a declaration of love

Love means something different to everyone, so it is particularly important to help your partner understand what you mean when you say "I love you." If saying that makes no difference to you or your relationship, why say it at all? There is no denying that for many people, those three little words hold immense power.

Society and entertainment have trained us to respond to those words. When we hear "I love you," we may envision commitment, support, dedication and trust. If you aren't equipped to provide these things to your partner, claiming love may do more harm than good.

Here are some questions to ask if your partner says those three little words:

- What does love mean to you?
- How do you think this will change our relationship going forward?
- What do you expect from me in return?

This last question is crucial. A declaration of love is a major thing for many people. They don't just claim it and expect nothing in return. If you aren't prepared to reciprocate, it is OK to say so! If your partner really loves you, they will be OK with not hearing it back—at least at first. If time goes by and you still have trouble saying it, a few things can be at play. You might be afraid of the commitment it represents.

You might not feel it is the right time. Or your feelings for your partner just might not be there.

Love may carry different meanings for different people, but it is real. Many say love is work and part of that is understanding what love means to your partner. That definition can change as you both grow and this is part of the magic of it. "Life affords you many opportunities to love different people, but it also can show you new ways to love the same person."

Part of wanting to be with someone is acknowledging that they will grow and change just like you will. It means not being selfish with your love. It means giving, not just receiving. If you aren't prepared to offer love or to try to understand it, you may be wasting your partner's time.

#5 – The addition of a new partner

Let's face it, love in the 21st century isn't your grand parents' love and it certainly isn't the way they'd define it either. More and more individuals are entering into consensual, non-monogamous relationships. The hallmark of these relationships is the understanding—shared by all partners involved—that physical and/or emotional bonds can be forged with other people.

These relationships take many forms and are known by many names. Keep in mind that these labels are flexible and subject to slight variations in meaning. "Polyamory' is the umbrella term that essentially means "to love multiple people." Multiple subcategories of polyamory exist, but they are all based on the principle that the relationship is not "exclusive." To reiterate, all partners must consent to this arrangement for the relationship to be considered polyamorous. Otherwise, it is just called cheating. Consent makes all the difference.

This book is not a guidebook for polyamorous or "open" relationships, but they must be addressed. While only 4% to 5% of people report engaging in polyamorous relationships, that number has been growing steadily in the past five years.

There is a difference between a relationship that begins as polyamorous vs. one that becomes polyamorous. In the first case, partners enter the relationship with their eyes wide open. They are all—hopefully—aware of the potential benefits and pitfalls. In the latter, partners must adjust to the new normal and this can take time. There is a major difference between talking about forming bonds with other people and actually doing it.

Polyamorous relationships—like any relationship—are complex and unpredictable. There is the possibility that an open relationship can undo itself through the introduction of someone new.

You may have received messages in life that say you can only love one person at a time. The concept of "true love" is still alive and well in many parts of the world. However, it is possible to love more than one person at a time since everyone you meet can bring out a different kind of chemistry within you, as stated in the Chenistry chapter.

Choices must still be made and they have ramifications. In an open relationship, you might meet someone whose chemistry really excites you. This might bring about a period of growth that pulls you away from your primary partner (some polyamorous relationships do not have primary partners, but most do). In this situation, you must face the reality that keeping your original relationship intact may no longer feel like the best choice. In this way, the addition of a new partner can precipitate the end of a relationship.

#6 – Marriage

Marriage may be the ultimate gesture of commitment. This stage is discussed fully in the "Chemistry" and "Therapy" chapters.

#7 – Having children

Not every relationship leads to this stage and let's be honest, not every relationship should. When children are introduced into a relationship, so much of what each partner has learned goes out the window because there is no manual of how to raise a child. Things you thought you know will be tested everyday and you will have to learn how to be a partner as a parent. It is important to keep in mind that while every person deserves to feel loved, not everyone will find that love in a romantic relationship. The unfair reality is that even people who have the most love to give may not find themselves able to bring children into the world.

Having children requires a level of commitment that some people lack. For this reason, it is critical to question everything about the relationship before making a serious effort at having children with your partner. This requires taking proactive steps to minimize your chance of heading down this road prematurely.

If you are thinking about having children with your partner, you must fully understand their level of commitment. Has your partner been there for you even when it wasn't easy? If your partner can't show up for you now, who do you think will be doing the work when it comes to raising kids?

It may be tough to ask the relevant questions at this stage of a relationship, especially if you have been together for years. However, an ounce of prevention is worth a pound of cure. It is worth repeating that communication is key!

You also need to ask yourself if you really want children. In your heart of hearts, is it truly the right move for you? Accidents happen and some women, tragically, are not given the choice about whether they get pregnant or if the child will be brought to term. If you are given the luxury of a choice, make the most informed decision you can.

A major component of this book is the necessity to question society's expectations. Many people, particularly heterosexuals, grow up surrounded by the assumption that one day they will get married and have children. The pressure of society is a potent force. It works its way into all our decision-making at a subconscious level. Think carefully about where your desire for children comes from. Do you feel undue pressure to have children now? Step outside yourself and question what you are doing as often as you can.

"What if you've made your bed, but you don't want to lay in it?" Such is the risk of blindly accepting society's expectations.

Of course, women face the particular challenges posed by their biological clocks. People are marrying later in life these days and, therefore, children come later as well. For many women, there is no way around this biological fact. Some women now choose to freeze their eggs, thus prolonging their child-bearing years. Women without the resources for such a procedure are still at the mercy of their bodies. The anxiety surrounding childrearing is real and powerful, but is it a reason to have kids before you are financially and mentally ready and before you meet the right person for you? That is up to the individual to decide.

If you are fortunate enough to have the flexibility to choose when and how to have children, here are some statements to consider:

- There is no law that says having children will make you happy. If you have the sense that something is missing in your life, children may distract you, but they won't necessarily satisfy it.
- Having children does not always bring partners closer. In fact, child-rearing presents a minefield of potential conflicts. If you and your partner can't agree now, just wait until kids enter the mix!
- Having children raises the stakes. If you are worried about the stability of your relationship now, things will only get more unpredictable. Raising children together requires a huge amount of trust. If this is an issue in your relationship, get to the bottom of it before introducing children into the mix. The hurt of a broken relationship will only be amplified with the addition of children. Reflect carefully before taking any drastic step in a relationship.

When and Where You Are

"Live life like you've done it before."

Hopefully, this chapter has highlighted the importance and inevitability of personal and relationship growth. If you enter into a relationship with the idea that you, your partner and your relationship will assuredly grow and develop, you not only increase the likelihood that the relationship will last but also safeguard the emotions of everyone involved.

Your relationship, to various degrees, affects those around you. A relationship is not a closed-loop; it generates externalities that your close friends and family cannot escape. When you act carelessly in your relationship, the spillover can be detrimental to others that you care about. Why would you not take every possible step to care for the psychological, physical and emotional health of your partner?

The start of a new relationship is the perfect time for meaningful self-reflection. Where are you personally, professionally, psychologically and emotionally? Are you in a place and time in your life with room for another person or are you only trying to meet your own needs?

Instead of searching for your "true love," acknowledge that this person will be different depending on where and when you both are in life. Most people begin relationships when they are young and still figuring things out. Be honest with yourself and your partner. Are you looking for a relationship for now or for years to come?

If your answer is not what your potential partner wants to hear, you cannot blame them for calling it quits. You will always be able to rest assured that you did your best to be honest just as long as you thought very carefully about why you arrived at the answer that you did.

Think about the crushes you had in your younger days. How many of these individuals are people you would still want to be with? Your answer is not a judgment on yourself or others; it is merely an acknowledgment that where and when you are in life will have an impact on who you think your "true love" is.

It is difficult to ascertain why relationships begin when they do. Perhaps it is enough to say that you both were just in the right place at the right time. When a relationship begins to falter, you may judge yourself and your partner harshly for the decisions you two have made. It may feel good at the moment to find some way to punish yourself or your partner, but this rarely leads anywhere positive.

Instead, focus on the factors at play: chemistry, growth and experience. Experience will be discussed in the next chapter.

In a way, parting ways can be a beautiful thing. Ideally, you have both acknowledged that each of you will be better off moving on. Unfortunately, many relationships do not end on such equal footing. Often, one partner wants to make it work while the other has had enough.

The questions and ideas presented in this chapter and all others are generally intended to be shared with your partner. Everyone needs some degree of privacy.

It can also be irresponsible to share every passing feeling that you have with your partner. Feelings change and develop even over a few hours. You might be hungry, tired, frustrated or overjoyed. These feelings have the potential to shape your immediate outlook on your relationship. If you share every single thought, fear, worry and concern with your partner, you run the risk of confusing them.

For this reason, it is important to keep track of how your feelings and thoughts develop over weeks and months, not just days and hours. If the feelings you have continue, then you know it's time to share them with your partner.

The importance of being present

Growth is a process that requires time. Hopefully, this chapter has illustrated how an otherwise happy and stable relationship can end because of the growth of one or both partners. While it may not seem appropriate to celebrate such an occasion, it need not be a tragic affair either.

When you shift your thinking to accommodate the fact that all relationships end, you can find contentment—even joy—when your relationship does conclude.

The danger here is that you may become overly preoccupied with the growth of your partner and your relationship. Any idea or concern that prevents you from feeling gratitude for the present must be confronted and examined.

If you are constantly worrying about how things will turn out, you aren't really living. If your waking life is consumed by work, screens, regrets and worries, then you aren't really living. You cannot be a strong and stable partner to your spouse if you cannot see them as they are in the present moment. Also, one day when you come around to want to focus on your partner, you risk replacing them with your *idea* of them. If you forget who your partner is or miss out on their growth because you're so busy, this will only lead to disaster; they will never measure up to your expectations and you also weren't being supportive of their growth.

A preoccupation with growth is a preoccupation with the future. The future hasn't happened yet! Sometimes, anxiety becomes so prominent that it seems real. The truth is, even if you have suffered trauma in the past, there is no guarantee you will suffer it in the future. Learn from your past when you can, but the best way to move forward is to have a attitude of gratitude for the present. The present moment always leads to the future, so enjoy the moment and know that you're on the right path.

Experience

"Experience is what you do and what happens to you. Growth is how you respond."

All relationships have rough patches, even ones that are healthy, supportive and beneficial to both partners. Much of this book is focused on how to talk to your partner and how to think and reflect on your relationship.

These two ideas are closely related. If you aren't thinking and reflecting carefully about your choices, how can you have a constructive conversation with your partner? Likewise, if all you do is ruminate about what could go wrong, your partner will have no idea what's going on inside your head. You'll drive yourself crazy before too long. While productive conversation and meaningful reflection are key to extending the life of your relationship, they aren't enough.

What is the missing piece?

This chapter focuses not on what we say or think, but on *what we do*. Our actions, choices and behaviors—over time—equal the sum total of our experience. Much of life is the result of factors that are outside our direct control. You didn't choose your parents, choose when or where you were born or choose the conditions of the greater world. All this is to say that life is full of surprises. Even the most detailed plans can fall through because of situations that you never could have predicted.

This chapter will focus on things you can do to extend the life of your relationship. As you read and process this information, keep in mind that you will never be able to fully predict the consequences of your actions. What you can do is make sure you have the best information possible while maintaining open communication with your partner.

Before we delve into how experience shapes individuals and their relationships, let's establish some important context.

Time: Friend or Foe?

> *"You cannot fully understand the power of experience without taking time into account."*

Humankind has not yet harnessed the power to manipulate time. We are caught in the current of seconds, minutes, hours, days and years that inevitably pass us by. Like death, the passage of time will affect human life in several ways.

Time ages us. Some people may have the resources or the genetic good fortune to delay the physical signs of aging, but it catches up with all of us if we're lucky. Time is relevant to each section of this book because time means change. Acknowledging the inevitability of change at the individual level is a requirement for a relationship to endure.

You must understand that if you are together for decades, you and your partner will both age physically. The day will come when you will notice wrinkles, sagging and other physical signs of age in yourself and your partner. This is not something to be ashamed of and it is not something you should hold against anyone. Aging is a natural part of human life and there is no escape.

When you are young, it feels like you have all the time in the world. You may be preoccupied with the future because of the great hopes and dreams that you hold. This is understandable, but you must also take time to find peace and gratitude in the present even when things aren't going your way. If you cannot find satisfaction in the present with your partner, there is very little chance that you will be able to find that satisfaction in the future.

Time also changes us mentally and psychologically. People tend to become wiser and more averse to risk as they age. Your feisty energetic partner will likely mellow out as they age. The same may very well be true for you. At the same time, don't go around hoping that your partner's annoying behaviors will disappear in the future. Previous chapters have information about how to determine when a behavior needs to be addressed and how to go about doing so.

For the reasons outlined above, experiences take on different meanings as you and your partner age. Over the years, you will hopefully build a shared context, and this will shape how you approach novel experiences. As you read through this chapter, consider how your stage of life affects how you interpret the information.

You cannot fully understand the power of experience without taking time into account.

Fixed and Moving Actions

"A life of delights and adventures doesn't just happen on its own."

No relationship is a fairy tale. When you approach relationships with fantastical and otherwise unrealistic expectations, you set yourself and your partner up to fail. See the "Growth" chapter for more about setting reasonable expectations. Even though most relationships will not reach that fairy-tale conclusion, there is something to learn from how a fairy tale—or any good story—plays out.

The famed writing teacher Rust Hills dispensed many pieces of advice over his long career as an editor and mentor. His work is focused on how to help writers write better stories. His ideas of *"fixed action"* and *"moving action"* provide a useful allegory to the way an individual's actions can affect a relationship.

"Fixed actions" include your routine behaviors, habits and quirks. If you have been living with your partner for a while, chances are they will know all your fixed actions. They know when you prefer to wake up and go to sleep. They know when you like to eat your meals and where. They know the chores you do (and the ones you don't do). They probably know the errands you run and the ones you prefer to put off. They know how you respond to the little stresses and inconveniences of everyday life. They know how you prefer to celebrate your successes. In short, your fixed actions are the way you typically behave amid various contexts. When you engage in a fixed action, you aren't going to surprise anyone.

In writing and storytelling, Hills points out that fixed action is how a reader gets to know a character. Fixed actions provide a baseline for the character to start from. At some point towards the beginning of a story—or a movie—the reader learns who the character is, what their priorities are and how they behave when things are in their normal state. In most stories, however, things don't stay normal for long.

Can you imagine a book or movie in which all you get to see are fixed actions? A character brushing their teeth, making the bed, moving through a typical day at work, cooking dinner and going to sleep? That story would most likely be extraordinarily boring. No one would want to read such a book or watch such a film.

"Moving actions," by contrast, are actions that surprise. They often happen in response to something unexpected. A character is often forced into moving action because their fixed actions are no longer viable. You can't brush your teeth if your kitchen is on fire. You can't go to work if the roads have flooded. Moving actions reveal a great deal about a character because moving actions often involve consequential choices. Moving actions show the world what a character—or individual—is like deep down. They reveal new dimensions that others usually don't get to see.

So what does this have to do with relationships? To put it simply, a life that consists solely of fixed actions is, in a sense, incomplete. If you've ever been in a long-term relationship, you are likely familiar with the sense of boredom that creeps in. Maybe you are in such a situation now. Have you asked yourself how much of your relationship consists of fixed actions? Can you make a list of moving actions from the past month? If you are struggling to come up with moving actions, then you may need to be proactive in making an adjustment. A life of delights and adventures doesn't just happen on its own.

Before you start beating yourself, keep in mind that we all need fixed actions in our lives. Most people thrive on structure and routine to help us order our lives and make sense of the world. The disturbing thing about fixed actions is that we often aren't aware of them. Our minds try to minimize the amount of conscious effort that we need to put forth. For this reason, our fixed actions often become unconscious. We aren't aware that we are doing them at least not in any meaningful sense. The beautiful part about being in a relationship is that there is someone close by that you can trust to help you notice these fixed actions. These actions can be innocuous—like sticking to a regular sleep schedule—but they can also be corrosive.

Actions, both fixed and moving, are closely tied to experience. While many experiences may be outside your direct control, making a commitment to moving actions will result in more purposeful, fulfilling experiences for yourself and your partner.

Passive and Active Experience

> *"If your relationship has hit a rough patch, try to see how your actions and behaviors have led you there."*

Now that we have drawn a distinction between fixed and moving actions, we must look at another dichotomy: *passive* vs. *active*.

Fixed actions provide stability and predictability to life while moving actions build character and lay the groundwork for new experiences. When you choose to engage in behavior that leads to a new experience, you are having an active experience. Active experiences create what some people might call "the spice of life." It can be as small as trying a new restaurant or surprising your partner with a home-cooked meal after a long day. It can also be as grand as a proposal of marriage or a vacation to an exotic location. Whenever you use your agency (your power to create change), you are engaging in a behavior that might lead to an active experience.

Passive experiences, by contrast, are ones that we do not choose. These can be positive, negative or neutral. If someone rear-ends your car at a stoplight, that is a negative passive experience. It happened to you and there was nothing you could have done to prevent it. Perhaps some new neighbors move in next door and you strike up a friendship. Maybe the government cuts taxes and you save some money.

You can probably already see that there is a lot of gray area in this distinction. Let's say your boss surprises you with a promotion at work. You didn't actively choose the promotion, but your hard work likely led to it. For this reason, it is often difficult to ascertain whether an experience is passive or active. It really depends on your point of view.

In many cases, it is up to the individual to frame the experience as passive or active. The distinction matters because causality matters. For some people, nothing is their fault. The world is out to get them. They take no responsibility for what happens to them. For a person like this, most experiences are passive. They are a rudderless ship on a stormy sea, existing entirely at the whims of the currents and the weather.

On the other end of the spectrum is the person who believes they are fully responsible for the experiences they have. They never need help from others because their life is great and they have worked hard to make it so. Every experience is active to a person like this because everything stems from the choices they make.

The sad thing about people in either of these categories is they are not usually consistent. People who assume they have full control over their experiences will be the first to blame others when things go wrong. Likewise, those who always play the victim will celebrate their own intelligence or hard work whenever something good actually happens to them. Most people tend to fall in the middle of these extremes. We tend to take most of the credit for the good experiences in our lives while sharing blame with others for many of the negatives.

So what is the healthiest way to view the experiences in your life? When it comes to relationships, you must hold two ideas in your mind at once. You must acknowledge and take some responsibility for how the relationship is going, but you must not put all the blame on yourself when things go wrong. In most healthy relationships, this viewpoint works well. There are exceptions, of course.

When it comes to abusive relationships—physical or emotional—the victim should not blame themselves for their partner's abusive behavior. No one deserves to live with the threat of violence hanging over their head. In fact, abusers will often blame the spouse for their own abusive behavior. This is done to alleviate guilt and justify their abuse. The distinction between passive and active experience is crucial here.

Ideally, you should strike a balance between framing your experiences as both active and passive. If your relationship has hit a rough patch, try to see how your actions and behaviors have led you there. When it comes to cases of lying and cheating, you need not assume responsibility for what your partner does, but you do bear part of the responsibility when it comes to moving forward.

Part of the commitment of a relationship is relinquishing full active control over your experiences. You must trust that your partner has your best interest in mind while working hard to earn and keep their trust.

Charting Your Experience

"Experiences provide the opportunity to self-reflect."

We can use the Fixed/Moving dichotomy in combination with Passive/Active dichotomy to get a snapshot of the current make up of your experiences. Actions and experiences work hand-in-hand to determine, in part, the kind of life you are leading. Each type of action/experience is important, but certain ratios are probably healthier and more fulfilling than others.

Passive Active

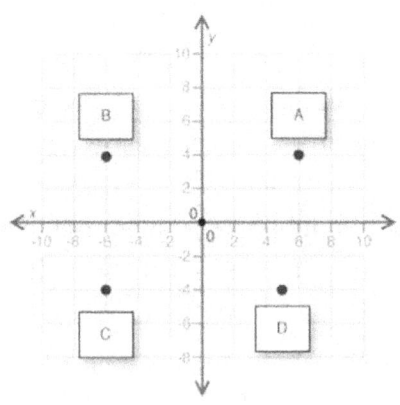

Moving   Fixed

A – Moving actions that lead to active experiences

These are those important "spice of life" actions. You and your spouse choose to take a road trip and explore a new part of the state or country. You choose to enroll in school to earn a new degree, opening you up to all kinds of new experiences, ideas and choices. These actions can be complicated or they can be simple. The trick is to find a balance. If your life is full of these types of experiences, you are probably living a pretty spontaneous and therefore unpredictable life. If you and your partner both thrive in this life, then you are probably set up for a pretty healthy dynamic. If your partner prefers predictable and stable, then you will have some negotiating to do.

You must also keep in mind that moving actions may have unpredictable consequences. You may end up in some sort of passive experience in which you don't have full control. Part of living spontaneously and open to new experiences means acknowledging that things won't always go as planned. If your life is completely lacking in these experiences, you—and your partner—are likely to experience boredom and that "stale" feeling that leads to problems.

B – Moving actions that lead to passive experiences

When you take a moving action (making an unexpected choice) that leads to passive experience, you are establishing a new habit, perhaps even beginning a new phase of life. You are making a commitment to change things by getting outside the status quo or making a fresh start. You decide to start working out and before long, going to the gym is second nature. It becomes such a part of your routine that you don't even need to think about it.

This can also be the situation that leads to the start of a new relationship or the end of an older one. Regardless of the scope of these actions, they change things and set you up on a new course. Such actions should only be taken after taking careful stock of your situation, doing your research and reflecting carefully on how the choice may affect others. This is also the time to seek advice or guidance.

In the context of a relationship, consider how your partner will be affected by such a change. Such actions should not be taken lightly unless they are very minor in scope.

C – Fixed actions that lead to passive experiences

In this case, your habits and unconscious behaviors lead you to experience the unexpected. These types of experiences are largely outside your control. You are staying in your lane, maintaining the status quo and yet the unexpected happens. Perhaps you lose a sense of agency.

If many of your passive experiences seem to stem from fixed actions, then you may be what some people call a *"vicious cycle."* Your normal behaviors are causing negative things to happen to you. Maybe you experience several breakups in a year. Maybe you find that you're having a hard time holding down a job. Maybe you are having frequent conflicts with those around you. If many of your experiences exist in this quadrant, it may be time to make a change.

On the other hand, what if your fixed actions are leading to many positive, yet surprising experiences? Maybe people often go out of their way to be kind to you. Maybe you get that promotion at work without putting forth any special effort. Maybe your daily life leads you into many unexpected, yet rewarding adventures and experiences. This may be because you have established healthy habits. You move through the world with kindness and compassion so the same comes back to you. If you have many of these experiences, consider yourself fortunate and enjoy them while they last.

However, such experiences also provide the opportunity to self-reflect. Is it really your habits and outlook that are resulting in so many unexpected, positive experiences? Some people just have the kind of appearance and personality that engenders goodwill in other people. Are you really doing anything leading to the positive things in your life or are you just "skating by?" If you aren't working particularly hard, it is safe to assume that your good fortune won't last forever. Enjoy such experiences, but be prepared for a change somewhere down the line. Take proactive steps now to safeguard the good things in your life and try to practice gratitude.

D – Fixed actions that lead to active experiences

Similar to the previous category, these experiences occur even when you don't take an active role in changing anything about your life. You are just trying to get by—keep your head above water—and yet you are constantly faced with new or recurring experiences that require all your attention. You are the person who is constantly putting out fires. Trouble seems to follow you everywhere. Maybe you are always playing catch-up at work and dealing with new issues that arise. Maybe you and your partner are always having new conflicts to manage. Maybe others in your life are constantly clamoring for your attention and assistance. Such a life can be hectic and stressful.

What types of habits have you fallen into? After a period of self-reflection and advice-seeking, try to make a change, even just a small one. Clearly, the path you are on is not sustainable.

On the other hand, some people thrive in such a life. Maybe you are content with a life full of tasks to accomplish, problems to solve and business to attend to. Maybe you are an active and valuable member of your family or community. Maybe you enjoy the active experiences that such a life requires of you. As is the case with the previous category, try to ascertain if your path is indeed sustainable long term. Take some time out for yourself and think outside the box.

Experiencing Life Together

"When we get accustomed to an experience, we protest for change."

When another person becomes entangled in your life, experience can get complicated. When is it OK to have your own experiences? When should you include your partner or spouse in your experience? There are so many questions to address, far too many for one book. Here are a few ideas and questions to keep in mind when experience intersects with relationships:

- No matter the stage of your relationship, having your own experiences is crucial to your well-being. Do not feel obligated to include your partner in every single experience you have.
- Shared experience, however, is incredibly important. We make time for what matters. If your partner—and your relationship—matters to you, strive

for a life full of active experiences for you both to share.

- Balance is key! Fixed action is not a bad thing. Ideally, you should understand how your habits affect your partner. Even if you have been together for a while and your habits haven't changed much, check in with your partner to see if they are happy with the way the relationship is going or if they are ready to make a change.
- Novelty leads to a rich life. Try new things both on your own and with your partner. It can even be something small like learning how to cook a new meal or visiting a new place. It doesn't have to be anything exotic or complicated!
- Keep track of your shared experience with a memory board or some other repository. Physical mementos become part of your shared legacy. Concert tickets, a brochure from that museum you visited, a souvenir from a trip, a menu from that new restaurant, a neat rock that you found on a hike. It all matters because you experienced it together.
- Get outside your comfort zone. If your partner likes foreign films, but you can't stand them, take the initiative to learn about them. Understand what your partner enjoys about the experience and remain open-minded to find enjoyment as well, if you can! Don't do it out of obligation; do it because you care about them.
- Share your experiences with friends or other couples. More often than not, the more the merrier! Other people add richness and excitement to experience. Sometimes, your partner just won't be enough and that is totally fine.

Experiencing the End

"When a relationship ends, that is a great time to reflect and learn from you experiences."

We return yet again to the theme of this book: All relationships inevitably end. Whether your relationships last a month, a year, five years or decades, you will carry the experiences with you for a lifetime. Unfortunately, a rich life of experience is not all that a relationship needs to thrive. As we have shown, it is just one of the factors. Without chemistry and growth, experience will fall short in extending the life of your relationship.

Ideally, you and your partner will be better off after the relationship ends. Maybe not right away, but in the long run. Once the emotional pain has worn off, take stock of the entirety of your relationship. When a relationship ends, that is a great time to reflect and learn from your experiences. There may never be a better time to reflect and record your thoughts. Perhaps you even learned some valuable lessons that you can carry into your next relationship. Write them down so you don't forget them.

For people of a certain age, particularly women, the end of a relationship means more than just the opportunity for a fresh start. Society and biology put a great deal of pressure on many people to continue with a relationship that should probably come to an end. If this is a factor for you, it's all the more reason to carefully reflect on what led to the end of the relationship. Figure out what you need in a relationship now and in the future. Take stock of your growth and use this to form your next steps.

Consider the reasons you got into the relationship in the first place. Did the person really exhibit the traits that you need in a spouse? A lasting relationship, for most, requires more than just a partner with good looks.

Remember to wait until your emotions have cooled to make any decisions about your present and future. Ending a relationship amid a fight can lead to regrets. When you are considering such a change—or processing in the wake of one—give yourself some time to return to a more typical emotional state.

At the end of a relationship, especially a bitter one, you may be tempted to eliminate everything in your life that reminds you of that person. This may be healthy, but keep in mind that some things cannot be purged. Acknowledge that you are a different person for having known your previous partner. Try to find some meaning and even gratitude for learning what you do or don't want in someone.

Self-Sabotage

"Emotions make us act impulsively."

Much of this chapter takes for granted the idea that both partners want the relationship to succeed. The actions of each may sometimes have unforeseen negative consequences, but partners rarely try to hurt each other, at least significantly. Unfortunately, there are times when one or both partners feel like their only option is to sabotage the relationship through hurtful words and actions.

Toxic relationships do not necessarily have to be physically abusive. It can be toxic just for the simple fact that a couple does not have tolerance for each other so there is constant negative exchanges, be it verbally or nonverbally, when the two interact. Why even stay together at that point? As discussed in the "Chemistry" chapter, some relationships just bring out the worst in one or both partners. Some prevent growth and encourage the development of bad habits. A toxic relationship is an almost constant source of stress and discomfort. In such situations, the relationship has typically run its course and should come to an end.

Unfortunately, relationships rarely end at the right time. Only after weeks or sometimes years of misery will one partner decide to call it quits. In such situations, a great deal of lying, arguing and perhaps even cheating has taken place. All these behaviors, at their core, are acts of sabotage. They may even be signs of desperation.

What if a person finds themselves in a healthy relationship and still acts in a self-sabotaging way? They break promises, act in a hurtful way towards their partner and resist efforts to repair the damage they caused. There are many reasons why a person may act this way. Perhaps they fear commitment and the way it may restrict their autonomy. Perhaps they have secret doubts about their partner that they are too afraid to say out loud. Perhaps they have just developed bad habits they can't break. The chapter, "Therapy," contains more information about these situations.

People don't always engage willingly in self-sabotaging behavior. In their own mind, they imagine that they have no choice and good intentions. These individuals have a fixed mindset. They may say to themselves, *"I am a certain way and I cannot change."* Therapy is one way that individuals can break a cycle of self-sabotage, but it doesn't happen overnight. It takes sustained effort and commitment to follow a careful plan for months, perhaps years. If a person is in love, if they care about their partner and relationship, they will take the steps necessary as long as they have sufficient resources.

Lets talk about it

"Give love a chance until you realize the person isn't for you."

Several sections of this book make reference to the Big Five Personality Traits model. Each trait falls on a continuum and every individual falls somewhere on each. The traits are:

- **Openness to experience:** Inventive/curious vs consistent/cautious
- **Conscientiousness:** Efficient/organized vs extravagant/careless
- **Extraversion:** Outgoing/energetic vs solitary/reserve
- **Agreeableness:** Friendly/compassionate vs challenging/callous
- **Neuroticism:** Sensitive/nervous vs resilient/confident

The acronym OCEAN describes this collection of traits. Every individual expresses these traits in different ways depending on the situation. For example, when it comes to conscientiousness, a person may be organized and efficient when planning a vacation, but they may be extravagant and careless when it comes to buying gifts for their friends and family. No one fits neatly into any one box.

Many individuals in relationships struggle with how to approach their spouse about anything related to behavior or personality. For example, maybe your partner has a habit of driving too fast and recklessly. Before you approach them about it, consider how your personality traits—and theirs—may be interacting in a way that is clouding your judgment.

Are you a particularly neurotic person when it comes to driving? Do you often find yourself nervous in heavy traffic? Do you know anyone who was injured or killed in a car accident? What about when it comes to agreeableness? Are you a person who often finds faults with others before noticing their strengths? Are you quick to criticize other people's decisions? If so, your level of neuroticism may be high—at least when it comes to driving. You also may be highly disagreeable or callous when it comes to interpreting and responding to the behavior of others. Your neuroticism and disagreeableness may be interacting in a way that makes you frightened and frustrated by your partner's driving. On the other hand, some people drive ridiculously fast and there is no doubt that there is a threat to, not only their life, but anyone in the car with them and on the road

Talk to a friend about what you observe when your partner is behind the wheel. Deliver the details as dispassionately as you can and resist editorializing about your feelings. If your friend thinks that your spouse really is a dangerous driver, it may be time to confront them about it. If, however, your friend thinks the situation is normal, you may need to do some work on yourself rather than asking your partner to change. Try to seek the counsel of a friend who knows you and your spouse; don't go looking for confirmation of your own bias.

The reckless driving scenario applies to situations in a relationship that is surrounded by biases when each partner grows intolerant of certain behaviors from their partner. Many relationships end because people become frustrated by their spouse's behavior. The frustration can build to the point of resentment and intolerance of each other. Before you let your relationship get to this point, take stock of your own personality traits and biases. Let some time pass and gather more data before rushing to judgment. Broach the subject when you and your partner are both calm. In this way, you help ensure that a strong relationship lives on.

Live or Let Die

"Settling now is one sure way to be unhappy in the future."

The options of men out there for women sucks. Hopefully you meet someone that's worth your time and treats you with care and respect. Just because most men out there aren't ready for commitment and do not know how to truly treat a woman doesn't mean women should ever settle for anything less than who they deserve.

If the person you're with shows you signs that they aren't for you, once again, I urge you to pack up your emotions and run the other way. The only thing waiting for you down that path is hurt and disappointment. You can't change people. We always have the hope to do so, but, in the end, "what you feel is what you get."

Are we making complaints to our significant other because we are calling them out on the things we see in them that we don't like? How many times would it take you to give up on calling them out on that particular issue? Depending on what the issue is, you can either ignore it or not. If you can live with it, then it is an issue that you were willing to accept as their downfall that you can live with.

Everyone has a different gauge of the things they will accept about their partner. It is based on things like our self-esteem, upbringing and what we've grown accustomed to. More importantly, it depends on how we love. If you love hard, then you may ignore all of someone's downfalls. Downfalls, in this case, refer to what a person lacks as a partner to your standards.

In relationships, as in life, the more issues you accept and choose to ignore increase your chances of being unhappy because you're not getting the things you like. "Settling now is one sure way to be unhappy in the future." There are couples that seem to have it all, but they aren't truly happy because they are in a relationship where they ignore a lot of things about their partner that makes them unhappy. Some of those issues were red flags in the beginning but the couple accepted them without evaluating if they were truly willing to accept certain things and now they have become problems.

What Are We?

"We're together but we're not together"

Sometimes, we end up in a kind of relationship that is so called "weird". People say, "We're together but we're not together". It's not weird. Often times it's because of compromise and fear of commitment and that type of a relationship is what works. Some of us want the sex but not the commitment. We want to stick to one partner at a time because it's safer and mixing that intimacy wouldn't feel as great compared to giving one person your all, even if it's not a full relationship. So you end up in a committed relationship that isn't a relationship. It sounds weird but it's still something. Some kind of connection exists. It's pretty much the new age of compromise when it comes to relationships.

It's not weird, it's just a byproduct of when people fear commitment.

So the other partner will compromise just to be with them for as long as it'll last.

Happiness

"If you aren't happy as an individual, you won't be happy in a relationship."

A strong relationship brings happiness, right? Well, it depends on what you mean by *"happiness."* According to Greater Good Science Center at University of California Berkeley, happiness has three main components:

- **Evaluative happiness:** How individuals view overall satisfaction with life.
- **Hedonic happiness:** How a person feels during any given moment, day to day
- **Eudaimonic happiness:** The degree of meaning that a person finds in life.

One issue with the way we talk about happiness is the vague way we define it. What does it really mean to be a happy person? It is more than just going around with a smile on your face. You've probably met many outwardly happy people who are filled with sadness and despair.

Taking a more holistic idea of happiness helps us keep things in perspective. Individuals of religious faith often report higher levels of evaluative happiness than non-religious people. However, their level of hedonic happiness may not be much different. If you are a person who generally feels blue much of the time, there might not be anything wrong with your life. You may be depressed, and this depression may cause you to see everything—your job, your spouse, your life—as hopelessly bad.

This is an important idea, but it doesn't hold true for everyone. What is true is this: There is no guarantee that a strong relationship will make you happier on each of the three happiness types. Being in a relationship with a person you love and care about may well raise your level of hedonic happiness, but is your spouse doing anything to affect your level of eudaimonic happiness? Some people find purpose and meaning in their love life, but this is certainly not the case for everyone.

There are no shortcuts to happiness or well-being. If you are lacking any of the three major happiness factors, a relationship will probably not be the way to solve the problem. If you are in a relationship, it also stands to reason that ending your relationship might not fix every problem you have. Many people find themselves in a damaging cycle. They enter a relationship, get a nice boost of hedonic happiness for a while, and may even raise their level of evaluative happiness for a time. However, as time goes on, the novelty of the relationship wears off.

If both partners are not putting in the effort, the level of hedonic happiness drops again. When the relationship ends, one or both partners may get a little boost of hedonic happiness as their "freedom" is returned to them. The happiness inevitably wears off and they go searching for another relationship. If you find yourself in such a pattern, you must do something to interrupt it.

Focus on finding meaning and purpose in life. Strive to meet new friends and engage in new kinds of experiences. Such richness will likely address the issues of happiness you are experiencing in a way that a relationship never could.

Life is undoubtably about our experience and enjoying them while we're here! Relationships are no different. Relationships are not the stories we constantly see in movies that are surrounded by fairy tales and false hope. There are no "happily ever afters" in life.

All relationships end in death after hopefully surviving the ups and downs of a relationship. All relationships will inevitably end but it's up to us to decide if we want to do everything we can, no matter what, to make it work. If we truly love our partner, the choices we make while in the relationship will extend its life and the longevity of it.

How do we deal with the end of a relationship when it comes? When our relationship ends, it's usually a sad ordeal because we are essentially losing someone close to us. Imagine getting super close with someone on so many levels, then deciding not to be together. It's almost like experiencing the death of a loved one. When someone dies, one of the worse thoughts is knowing that you'll never be able to see that person again.

The ending of a relationship is slightly similar. Imagine not ever speaking to this person that you used to date because now that the relationship is over, you are, in a sense, dead to each other. Unfortunately, death is the end all be all but with a breakup, the person still exists but now you must walk this earth as if they never did. What a sad thought. There is no wonder why people experience grief during a breakup. In time, things do get better, but until then you'll be a wreck. It's best to think of what you learned and how you both helped each other. Even though the situation is sad, you'll be able to look back one day and know that you are better because of it. This will be discussed further in the last chapter.

We like to experience life. In a relationship, we still experience life but as a couple, and rightfully so. After some time of doing the same thing over and over, you will tire of it even if it is a great relationship. It'll be a routine that you have become accustomed to. It's similar to constantly eating the same type of food. Experiences are more enjoyable the less you experience them.

Constant stimulation from the same experience will begin to have less of an effect on us. This is why we naturally get bored in a relationship. You'll even hear couple say they need to add spice to their relationship. Hopefully, they are successful on adding new things. If not, then one or both individuals will cheat, seek attention from elsewhere or break up. Also, let's face it. For some people, cheating is a choice they make even when they get the attention, love and care from their partner. Some people are just curious about experiences with others even while they're in a great relationship. You must find out what kind of partner you have. Sometimes it's ok to ask prying questions and encourage them just to be sure you're getting the most honest answer. But if you always have to use this tactic, maybe your are not trusting of your partner or maybe they're not right for you.

If you do stay together, the changes you make can only last for a certain period because of the experience factor. Over time, we get used to the same person. The chemistry and fundamental foundations of your relationship have already been set. When you try to spice things up, it's hard to accomplish because you both have established boundaries within the relationship and how you interact with each other. You know certain things your partner would and wouldn't do and they know the same about you. If they try something new, it can only last so long before you both become your natural selves again. Changing is worth trying to save your relationship. It would help if you both tried it, but over time you'll go back to your natural ways of interacting with each other.

In a relationship, the intention is to be with someone you feel right with. When you're in a relationship, you want to do things with your partner to be happy and share the moment together. You can do many different things together as a couple, as you should. The problem is when you rely on your partner to make you happy.

Happiness starts from within. Feeling unhappy will pour into your relationship. Even when you have great moments day to day, you will have an underlying feeling of negativity. You will be occupied and happy in certain moments, but most times you'll feel empty. This will lead to arguments, big or small, and a negative situation always waiting to happen.

When you're not happy as a person, you will walk around with a chip on your shoulder, ready to explode and unleash your frustration on the next person who rubs you the wrong way. These are signs that it's best for you to be alone and focus on becoming happy as an individual. It's best to do this before getting into a serious relationship because it'll either result in your relationship ending sooner or taking a break. But be warned, taking a break is very risky. If you're already in a relationship and you need time to assess yourself, tell your partner and be open and honest about what it is that's causing the feeling or where it stems from.

A break symbolizes that you both acknowledge there are issues that you both are going through and experiencing together. Taking a break is supposed to give you both time to reflect and approach the situation differently after thinking about it. How mature you both are and how invested you still are in the relationship will determine what direction the relationship will go.

Some people use a break as an excuse to date and flirt with others because they mostly feel deprived of others and want to experience the world. Perhaps they just want to meet someone new who will treat them better than their partner. This doesn't mean that they'll cheat, but it does mean that now they will talk to other people without feeling guilty.

Unfortunately, sometimes just a conversation with someone else can make you feel like you've been missing a lot. Some might have sex with the first person they have a great conversation with. Some may take longer and some not at all. When it comes to human connection and experience, we take chances even if we're in a relationship because we ultimately live for experience. When there's a break, it's safe and OK to think that the relationship is over because of the natural flow of events when one or both partners meet new people. They'll enjoy the experience vs. being stuck in a relationship that isn't working. Chances are if it's not working, you should let it go. Forget about a break. *"A break means a breakup!"* A break can be very helpful but it's best that the couple talk about what's ok and not ok during the break.

Everyone needs to understand everything it takes for a relationship to work. While you get what you want out of the relationship, make sure your partner is getting what they need while you give the relationship what it needs. This includes attention, compromise and, above all, time. Time is everywhere and in everything we do in life. The choices we make in the present will always create our future. In a relationship that works, partners give attention to each other in an active and positive way. The way that attention is given will create a better tomorrow.

Cheating

"You did nothing wrong by asking to be treated right."

There are many ways that a relationship can end, so why devote a whole chapter to just one?

Nowhere in this book will you find the claim that relationships are easy. Contrary to what may be depicted in movies and peoples perfect couple social media profiles, relationships require effort. You need to work at it if you want it to last.

While there are exceptions, no relationship is sustainable on autopilot. Two individuals may have excellent chemistry, yet are unable to persevere through a difficult challenge. One of this book's aims is to show that relationships depend on several factors, not just chemistry or compatibility. It is only human to mentally envision your perfect partner and compare them to everyone you meet. It is not so common to envision a scenario in which you and your "perfect" partner need to resolve a conflict or make a difficult decision about the future of your relationship. Now more than ever, people expect people and their relationships to come perfectly packaged. This is not realistic. As technology exponentially evolves and makes things easier for us, people expect everything in their lives to be just as easy.

There are many reasons why people cheat, but it doesn't help to try to name them all. The reason is this: A person doesn't cheat unless they feel it is justified. The issue isn't "why" do people cheat, but rather "how does a person rationalize cheating in the first place?" Only the most vindictive, insecure person will cheat on their spouse with lack of care, consideration and integrity.

Everyone is the hero of their own story. Most people who cheat likely see themselves as the victim. The victim of a neglectful spouse. The victim of circumstances beyond their control. The victim of their past experiences and traumas. Not only is this victim mentality unhelpful, but it can also hurt others and perpetuate a cycle of damaging behavior that may not end when a new relationship begins.

Whether a person cheats to hasten the end of a bad relationship or just to satisfy their urges, the reason isn't important. The important thing is to understand how cheating could affect the spouse being cheated on and the relationship, whether the cheater gets caught or not. If you were ever cheated on, do not accept anything your partner says without question. The more you know, the better you're protected because you can make an accurate judgment based on what has happened. If your partner makes a selfish decision, address it. "You did nothing wrong by asking to be treated right!"

What Is Cheating?

"Cheating is the worse action against your relationship because it's reaching outside of what you two have built together only to destroy it."

Most people define cheating as engaging in physical intimacy with another person without their partner's knowledge or consent. As with all terms, there is some gray area. A cheating behavior in one relationship may not be considered as such in another relationship. To some couples, dancing with other people at a nightclub is considered cheating. Other couples may agree that such behavior is totally fine, depending on the type of dancing it is. Some forms of dance are sexual by nature but depending on what types of culture you're used to, it may or may not be ok.

When it comes to emotional intimacy, the same variation applies. Emotionally cheating is rarely described as cheating but it can be treated similarly. Here's a way to look at it. Does your partner know about it? If they don't know about your emotional involvement with another person, ask yourself why you haven't told them. Cheating is considered by most people to be a transgression. It is something that is very rarely justified.

Married couples in the United States reap hundreds of benefits that nonmarried couples do not get to enjoy. There are financial incentives in the form of tax advantages, savings advantages and dozens of others. Married couples have an easier time qualifying for the credit to buy a home or make other major purchases. If one spouse is unemployed, they can easily qualify for their employed spouse's health care plan.

Couples retain decision-making rights for their spouse should they become incapacitated.

According to the U.S. Government Accountability Office, there are over 1,100 statutory provisions—laws—in which marital status is a determining factor when it comes to conferring rights, privileges and benefits in society. Basically, the government gives every American 1,100 reasons to get married. While there are undoubtedly certain privileges that one relinquishes when marrying, the benefits far outweigh them. The caviat to that is as long as you stay married. We've all heard the nightmare horror stories of people that go through a divorce. The biggest downside being the financial loss.

With all those benefits, it is difficult today to acknowledge that these rights were denied to many millions of LGBTQIA people for so long.

In the context of marriage, cheating has major financial and legal implications. Adultery—a married individual engaging in sexual intercourse with a person other than their legal spouse—is actually a crime punishable by fines or jail time in 21 states. Even in states where adultery is legal, a cheating spouse can lose the rights and privileges that would normally be afforded to them in a divorce. Cheating can be used as a determining factor when a court makes decisions regarding alimony, spousal support and even child custody. In some states, spouses have legal recourse to sue their cheating partner—and the other person—after the marriage is dissolved. And yet, cheating is still quite prevalent.

The legal ramifications of cheating for nonmarried people are limited. Instead, the consequences are primarily emotional and psychological. This may be another reason why cheating is more prevalent in relationships that do not hold the legal standing of marriage. When a couple isn't legally married, it is much easier to rationalize an action that risks the relationship.

The precise behaviors that define cheating are different for every couple. At the end of the day, it may come down to attention. Implicit in most relationships is the idea that each partner will, to a certain degree, give their significant other priority when it comes to making decisions about how to direct attention. When a person is important in your life, you naturally show them more attention. When you claim to love a person without giving them the attention they deserve, it is often described as taking your partner for granted. Your actions imply that you think your partner will be there forever despite how little attention you give them.

It is fair to interpret this behavior as a warning sign. If a new person enters your life and you find yourself giving them more attention you would normally pay to your spouse, then you may be at risk of cheating. In the eyes of your partner, the cheating may already have begun. You might not even care that you're on the verge of breaking your loyalty but at least mention it to your partner before hand or talk to your friends about the feeling. Be active in trying to avoid cheating just as active as you were to create that terrible opportunity. Chasing and desiring a new partner is one thing but doing so while you already have someone is disrespectful.

Who Cheats?

"At the end of the day, everyone has the potential to cheat."

Many people may be under the impression that cheating is a common occurrence and they may actually be right. The divorce rate accounts for people getting a divorce but, most times, it doesn't mean that the people that were married last year are filing for a divorce the following year. It is a figure that is derived from the amount of people married this year versus the amount of people getting a divorce this year. It's a testament to the fact that it will eventually happen. Just like the divorce rate, cheating doesn't constantly happen in every relationship. It happens eventually. Some people don't cheat at all. There some relationships that has a partner that cheats constantly. There are others that may cheat once or twice. Point is, it happens. The first major studies on cheating, completed by Dr. Alfred Kinsey in the 1940s, indicated that about 50% of married men and 26% of women admitted to being unfaithful. Many decades have passed since Kinsey's pioneering studies, but today, cheating is just as prevalent as it was 80 years ago. Taking into account that standard research methods likely result in an underestimation of how many people cheat, today's research indicates that perhaps 70% of men have cheated on their spouse.

There are many factors at play here. The chance of a person cheating can be affected by any of the following:
- Income level
- Religious affiliation
- Geography
- Age

- Gender
- Length of the relationship
- New Desires
- Personality

This final factor, according to some 2015 reporting by data journalist Mona Chalabi, may be the most influential in determining whether a person will cheat. A person who is more open-minded, adventurous and sexually confident is far more likely to cheat than a person without these characteristics.

Another consistent finding is that men tend to cheat far more often than women among most demographic groups. There are many possible explanations for this. One study found that wealthy men tend to cheat more as their wealth grows. However, poor women tend to cheat more than poor men among certain demographics. These findings indicate that socioeconomic status may be an important factor as well.

Interestingly, women tend to have a more capacious—broader—definition of what cheating means. An anonymous YouGov poll from 2015 indicated that over 70% of women viewed a flirtatious text message as cheating while only 59% of men felt the same.

There is also some research indicating that children of parents who committed infidelity are more likely to cheat as well. A 2015 study published in the *Journal of Family Issues* found that these individuals are about twice as likely to cheat as those whose parents remained faithful.

At the end of the day, everyone has the potential to cheat. Since there are so many factors at play, it doesn't help to prejudge a person's propensity for cheating before getting to know them.

The Excuses

"Without meaningful new experiences to inject excitement into a relationship, partners usually grow apart."

When it comes to cheating, the reasons behind it should not be the focus. When we focus on the "why," we end up focusing on the past. It becomes easier for the cheater to tell themselves a story about why it was OK for them to cheat. They tell this story to friends and new partners and they suddenly become the hero. It doesn't help the person who was cheated on. Cheating is cheating no matter the reasoning. It is such a selfish act! It can lead the person cheated to blame themselves for their partner's infidelity and they will carry this insecurity into their future relationships. They may make reactive decisions based on fear instead of responding thoughtfully to issues of trust and honesty.

Let's just say that cheating results from problems of chemistry and experience. Being in a relationship means, in a sense, limiting yourself to the chemistry you share with your partner. As time goes on, this chemistry becomes routine and even monotonous. Without meaningful new experiences to inject excitement into a relationship, partners usually grow apart.

The reasons for cheating are also pretty uninteresting most of the time. Many people cheat because it is a thrill. Most of us get a bump of adrenaline when we break the rules; transgression can be fun and even sexy. For people who are unhappy with the contents or trajectory of their lives, the negative effects of cheating do not outweigh the thrill as temporary as it might be. Instead of focusing so much on why people cheat, we will focus instead on how cheating affects you and your partner.

Cheating: Risks and Impact

"They're literally risking the health and well-being of the person they have committed to love and protect."

When one partner cheats, it will inevitably affect their partner. Cheating is an act of betrayal, and every betrayal—whether the other partner finds out or not—has long-reaching consequences for everyone involved.

Physical health

Paramount to every consideration of cheating is the physical risk it places on the cheater's partner. This may sound prudish, but the fact is there is no such thing as safe sex at least the way most people define it. While condoms prevent the transmission of diseases like HIV, gonorrhea and syphilis 99% of the time, there is a big difference between 99% and 100%. To clarify, this relatively small chance of failure should not prevent a person from enjoying the pleasures of sex. Sex should only occur between consenting adults who understand the risks and if they are both single.

All sexual behaviors carry some risk. Even kissing can transmit herpes, mononucleosis and minor infections like the common cold. Even if both partners seem healthy, there is the potential that they may be infected but asymptomatic. Again, these factors alone need not instill fear. Most common sexually transmitted infections are easily treatable and have no long-term consequences. Still, there is always a risk.

Genital herpes and genital warts, to name two, have no cure and they can be transmitted merely through skin-to-skin contact. A condom provides some defense against these infections, but not a complete defense. But even herpes is just a skin condition if you think about it. It isn't life threatening.

For many sexually active individuals, particularly men who have sex with other men, the risk of HIV infection is still a reality. Breakthroughs in preventative treatments have significantly reduced the risk of contracting the virus for individuals on a pre-exposure prophylactic (PreP) regimen. Those who take a PreP daily reduce the risk of contracting HIV from an infected partner by more than 99%. Again, the risk is not zero, but it is significantly reduced. An individual's HIV status no longer carries the stigma it did 10 years ago, and with good reason because of so much research and development. All this is to say that cheating on your partner puts them at risk. Even the safest, most careful sex can transmit infection. Let's also be honest, when engaging in the act of cheating, or sex in general, people don't always use condoms which raises the rate of infection drastically.

A spouse cheating on their significant other is betrayal. It becomes an even more serious transgression if the cheater chooses to be physically intimate with their significant other after cheating. They are literally risking the health and well-being of the person they have committed to love and protect. Aside from direct physical violence, it is difficult to imagine a crueler betrayal.

Loss of trust

After a partner cheats, the best-case scenario is that the cheater quickly confesses. By the time this happens, though, trust has already been damaged. The cheater has no right to claim the moral high ground just because they did the mature thing and 'fessed up to their behavior. For many people, there is no fixing a relationship damaged by a cheating spouse. The cheater has no right to blame their spouse for ending things. In fact, going on a break immediately to reflect on the damage may be best for everybody involved, if the the relationship isn't over immediately.

Trust is relevant to every chapter in this book, but the "Growth" chapter explores it in full. Without trust, a relationship is doomed to fail.

When trust is damaged, there are ways to repair it. The chapters on experience and therapy offer concrete steps that a person can take if there is the willingness to stay in a relationship damaged by a loss of trust. The only way this is possible is if both partners still want to make the relationship work. If a partner cheats, the ball is no longer in their court. They may want to stay together, but if their spouse is unwilling, there really isn't a way forward.

Emotional and psychological health

A person may not intend to hurt their partner by cheating, but harm will almost certainly come. Even if the cheater isn't putting their partner's health in danger through undisclosed sexual encounters, the emotional and psychological damage can be severe.

A betrayal of trust is a trauma and like all trauma, it takes time and effort to overcome. When a person cheats, they place an immense burden on their partner. Their partner may be plagued by guilt. They may blame themselves for the cheating. Such guilt may be unfounded, but it can take years to let go of it.

A person may need to invest financially in moving on from a relationship damaged by a loss of trust. Therapy costs money. Finding a new place to live costs money. Decoupling from the partner they trusted takes time, money and other resources. If a person doesn't have family or some other strong support system, they are forced to deal with the situation alone. They have to deal with the consequences of their partner's behavior. These cascading impacts can make the hurt linger for months, even years.

When a person cheats, they are essentially saying that they don't care about all the suffering that they may cause. A cheater shows little concern or care for the potential consequences that their partner will now have to deal with.

Future relationships

A person who experiences cheating in a relationship will likely carry the experience through to future relationships. Aside from emotional and psychological trauma, there are additional hidden effects that could negatively impact a person.

Cheating is a sign that there is something wrong with a relationship. In a twisted way, cheating is a "solution" to the problem. Cheating can provide an outlet that gives a person a sense of life and satisfaction. By improving their happiness, they may imagine that their relationship will run more smoothly. Cheating is like a pressure release. On the other hand, cheating can be a roundabout way to end a toxic relationship. Rather than just have a hard conversation, the person acts out their dissatisfaction in the hopes that their partner will put an end to the relationship for them.

Either way, cheating can be considered an unhealthy coping mechanism. If a person always resorts to cheating when a relationship gets tough, they never learn any other skills or strategies for resolving conflicts or overcoming the problems presented by chemistry. They never learn how to speak their concerns aloud to their partner. They never learn the satisfaction of moving past a conflict together. These people risk falling into a vicious cycle where they give themselves no choice but to cheat their way out of a relationship.

But What if They Never Find Out?

These are probably some of the most common expressions that people use to rationalize cheating.

- *It was just one time.*
- *I felt so bad about it, I'll never do it again.*
- *There is no way my partner will find out.*
- *I've covered my tracks.*
- *It's no big deal because no one got hurt.*

People keep secrets for all kinds of reasons. Sometimes, they are doing it in the best interest of their partner. Whether this is morally right or wrong isn't the discussion here. The important thing about cheating is that it happened whether the cheater's partner finds out or not.

When a person hides their infidelity, they may feel good at first. They think they can put the whole thing behind them. However, you don't just keep a secret once. It takes effort to keep a secret over time. You may find yourself avoiding certain topics with your partner. You may be short with your partner and get agitated when they ask certain questions. You may find yourself forced into a lie if your partner confronts you directly. Over time, contempt for your partner may creep in. You may start to see your partner as gullible or oblivious. Harboring such feelings for the person you are committed to will not lead anywhere good. Keeping a secret often requires people to tell *someone*—a friend, a co-worker, a family member. Forcing someone to be complicit in your lie only spreads the hurt to more people like a virus.

Cheating is like altering the DNA of a relationship. It simply cannot be undone. Not even with time, growth or experience. It doesn't matter if your partner never finds out.

Cheating in an "Open" Relationship

"Open relationship" is not synonymous with "freedom from commitment."

Being in an open relationship doesn't mean that cheating is impossible. Every open relationship has its own rules and expectations. The relationship is only open if both partners consent to and agree with the terms. For example, a couple may decide that physical intimacy with others is permissible as long as advance notice is given and safe sex practices are followed.

If one partner doesn't follow the protocols, it is easy to see how the other partner might feel a sense of betrayal. Obviously, if one partner is hiding their experiences with other partners—or lying about them—another breach of trust has occurred. Many people fantasize about how freeing an open relationship will feel. They don't often think about the conversations and negotiations that need to take place for an open relationship to work.

"Open relationship" is not synonymous with "freedom from commitment." Partners in an open relationship can and should be just as dedicated to their primary partner as those in traditional relationships.

Cheating and Growth

"You want to find love, but you're never serious!"

This chapter has focused primarily on the negative impact of cheating, but there can be a silver lining. When cheating ends a relationship, there is an opportunity for growth through self-reflection.

A breakup that results from cheating can be a wake-up call. Fear of making the same mistake twice can cause people to seek help through therapy, critical self-assessment and reflection. One of the best long-term responses to mistakes and hardship is to make meaningful, positive change. A cheater does not have to be a cheater forever. Assuming a fatalistic attitude is not the best way to move forward or atone for mistakes.

It is important to wait until emotions have cooled before taking any drastic steps or beginning the process of healing. No one can act rationally when they are angry, hurt or afraid.

For individuals who have suffered the betrayal of an unfaithful spouse, there are multiple ways forward. While it isn't helpful to blame yourself for your spouse's cheating, you must accept some responsibility for the relationship as a whole. Relationships are rarely so one-sided. There are certain cases where a person really is the unfortunate victim of their partner's bad behavior, but more often than not, a relationship is the product of all people involved.

Denying your role in a breakup—even if it was precipitated by your partner's cheating—is not a healthy way to move forward. You run the risk of assuming the victim mentality and abdicating all responsibility for the health and well-being of your future relationships.

It is possible to acknowledge responsibility without placing unnecessary blame on yourself. There is nothing shameful about recognizing your own shortcomings. It will make you a better partner once you've learned from it.

In this book, we have used the metaphor of a relationship as a living organism to highlight how a relationship is more than the sum of its parts. When two people make that commitment, they are creating a new kind of life. A relationship is not a child, but it must be cared for if it is to grow, thrive and endure. A cheating spouse is signaling that the relationship isn't worthy of care and attention. They signal that their selfish desires are more important than what they have built with their partner.

Eventually, if your partner decided to meet new people behind your back, they'll begin to realize how much fun they are having because naturally they've been missing "something." That "something" is human interaction. It's only natural that anyone would feel happy about meeting new people because they've been experiencing one kind of chemistry for so long. This is what lays the groundwork for people to cheat and why relationships can ultimately end sooner.

The truth is, there are people made to be in a relationship and others who are not. Most of us like to think we are because it's part of society and our culture. The ones who have a hard time being in a relationship are not made for it. It's a cookie-cutter ideal that tells you how relationships should be and how you should exist in them. Question everything! Do you want to be in a relationship because you truly want to? Or is it because that's all you know based on what you've been taught from birth?

This certainly goes against the idea of what a relationship represents, but this is true when you think about relationships with partners that have experienced cheating. Some even take a break and without telling their significant other, they hook up with people or go on dates purely for entertainment and fun. The date doesn't replace the person they are with, but it certainly provides a break from the relationship and experiencing the type of chemistry they've been used to receiving from their partner.

Coupled with the fact that as humans, we live to experience things, cheating is more common because it's a thrill to experience new encounters with others. Dating and hooking up becomes a sport and having sex is scoring, pun intended. You can give your partner the best relationship life can offer and they will still cheat because it has become a part of what they do.

Again, it is a selfish act when you're in a relationship with a partner who says cheating isn't OK. Sex with others is only OK if you're single or in an open relationship and agree to and follow the rules that you've both accepted. At that point, it isn't cheating unless you break one of the rules.

Here are a few questions to ask yourself to get an idea if relationships are for you:

- Would you ever cheat on your partner?
- Do you feel like you're missing out on opportunities to meet new people?
- Do you often flirt with people you find attractive?
- Do you truly want to be in a relationship?
- Are you in a relationship but feel stuck and obligated to your partner because of your history together?
- Are you connected and honest with your partner but you hide your true desires?

If you answered "yes" to any of these questions, maybe you should reconsider being in a relationship. Why should your partner be a bystander to what you truly want? If you want to hook up with people and you're not completely honest with yourself, and your partner, about your commitment to the relationship, then why bother being together? Save them the heartache if you know you don't want to be in a relationship.

Another thing to consider. Relationships are not for you if you feel like every person you meet is like a different vacation and some are better than others but you accept it because you're traveling. It may not be about having 100 partners or a thousand. It's about the experience for you. If sex isn't included, it's ok. The world in variety is the goal. Sex is not necessary for a good time. For people like this, if you settle down before it's your time to do so, you will be miserable and hurt people along the way. Stay single and be true to who you are. Have compassion and integrity for others.

Even if you sabotage your relationship on purpose, don't you realize it would take way less effort to be honest and single? Be honest about the way you feel and what you want? If you truly love them and want to be in a relationship, then come clean and tell them how you feel and what your thoughts are. Maybe they'll help you to discover your commitment side. Maybe they can help guide you back to them. But do not use this tactic and still be dishonest in your actions.

If you messed up in a relationship and the relationship ended, let it go. We all know you don't know what you got until it's gone. Often, as time goes by, the person that ruined the relationship tends to reach out to their ex-partner. Yes, the one they left broken-hearted or hurt.

It's understandable that some people will remain in contact with their ex-partners and some may even stay friends. But, if you're reaching out with the intentions of catching up to let your ex know how much you have changed and improved as a person, get over yourself! Especially knowing good and well how much you've hurt them or left them scarred in any kind of way.

Think of it this way. If you're reaching out to update them about you, it's still about you and you're clearly still self-absorbed. If you're calling your ex to let them know about life and only asking about theirs because conversation warrants an exchange, don't bother them. Let it go. You both learned from that past relationship, so why talk if it'll only be a reminder of what failed?

Now, if you're reaching out to somehow correct everything and swoop them off their feet, then take your chance. Just consider the fact that when your ex needed you to be a better partner, you failed. Although there is no guarantee they'll still be interested, at least your change of heart is being expressed and that's all that you can do.

Sexualized Bodies

"There's a difference between appreciating beauty and sexualizing a body."

There is a difference between appreciating beauty and sexualizing a body. The appreciation of form and beauty—often referred to as aesthetics—is an effort to seek out what makes a body special. It is more than just a snap judgment. A fine work of art, be it a painting, a sculpture or even a film, takes time, energy, thought and reflection to truly appreciate. The same goes for people.

On the other hand, sexualizing a body means to view it only as an object for pleasure. This is what is meant by the term "objectify." When a man objectifies a woman (or any other person), he sees her as a means to an end. An empty vessel whose purpose is only to help him achieve sexual gratification. It's as if having sex is the victory, so women are conquered and then thrown away. Objectification requires neither time, effort nor imagination. It is a selfish act undertaken without care for the other person.

As is the case with almost every facet of human life, there is no black and white. There is a wide spectrum between sexualization and appreciation. It is possible to deeply appreciate a woman's beauty while also becoming excited by the prospect of sexual consummation. Likewise, it is possible to appreciate the beauty of another person without feeling sexual desire. Society still has a difficult time with this dichotomy.

When it comes to relationships, appearance matters. There are no two ways about it. It is perfectly reasonable and human to care about how your partner looks. People should never be shamed for "wanting what they want," so to speak. However, how many people actually take the time to try and understand where their feeling of sexual attraction comes from? Ideals of beauty change with the times, but in modern society, the effects of technology and social media have put these changes into overdrive.

Social Media

"Pictures can say a thousand words, but never the full story."

People often marvel at how easy it has become to access massive quantities of information via the internet. You can learn about pretty much any topic under the sun. However, the most remarkable thing about the digital age is not just the amount of information out there, but the ease with which people can now create and share their own media with the rest of the world.

There is a new term that we can use to describe the world of social media: "hyperreality." It refers to the blurring line between fantasy and reality. When we scroll through a person's Instagram or Tik Tok, we think we are seeing them as they really are. However, this is never the case. A person's social media profile is curated, meaning that the person picks and chooses exactly what parts of themselves to show to the world and which parts to keep hidden. It is so easy to spend hours scrolling through pictures of people with "perfect" features. The "perfect" face, the "perfect" body, the "perfect" posterior. Full lips, sculpted eyebrows, gorgeous eyes and hair. We look at these images and they change the way we see the world. They change the way we see ourselves and they change the way we see other people.

How much time do you spend comparing the reality of your life to the hyperreality of an influencer's social media posts? It is even worse than comparing apples to oranges. Real life can never measure up to hyperreality.

If you are taking all your cues from social media about what to look for in a partner, you are setting yourself up for a lot of pain and disappointment. Even worse is the pain that you will put other people through. They will never be able to live up to your idealized view of what they "should" look like and how they should be.

The Sexualization of Women

"A man who is consumed by social media's hyper-real definition of sexualized beauty will less than likely be interested in an average or natural woman."

Many men perpetuate the traits they want in a woman: a big backside, big boobs and much more. But these are all physical attributes that are heavily sexualized by our culture. If men really took the time to answer *"What do I look for in a woman?"* they will actually begin to describe character traits. All the physical features will be in the background. As a result of years and years of praising the sexualized features of women, now most of the world perpetuates and is convinced that such features are beauty. Some Instagram models and celebrities push the same idea of what they've been convinced to be beautiful. Men have convinced a lot of women that beauty and sexualization are the same things: "big lips, a big butt and huge fake boobs."

Because of social media, the plastic surgery industry has exploded in wealth and influence. Many women—and men, too—have set unrealistic goals for their appearance. The fact is there are a lot of Instagram influencers and models that have enhanced their bodies through surgery. The proportions of their bodies and the structures of their faces are extraordinarily uncommon. There are no magic pills to make a man taller or a woman's breasts larger without surgery. A man cannot bench press his way to a sculpted face and most women cannot squat their way to a giant butt.

However, plastic surgery and other medical procedures—liposuction, gastric bypass, implants—can alter a person's appearance. These procedures are often prohibitively expensive for most people, turning "beauty" into something that only the rich and privileged can access. But, now more than ever, there are more and more places to get those procedures done for a lot cheaper. Unfortunately, the cheaper the procedure, the more of a health risk it is. The low price comes with a high cost of life or death, which some people are willing to gamble with.

For men, the flip side to that is they see these unrealistic images of women and begin to find them more appealing than the real deal. They may have a partner who lives a healthy lifestyle or works hard on their appearance through exercise. Unfortunately, their partner's efforts will make no difference. A man who is consumed by social media's hyperreal definition of sexualized beauty will less than likely be interested in an average or natural woman.

It is reasonable to wonder why so many women choose to emulate the appearance of the Instagram model in real life. It's not like men are forcing women to get surgery or spend hours in the gym. Keep this in mind: Everyone wants to attract a good partner and have a stable relationship. If society is constantly bombarding men and women with unattainable images of beauty, it changes everyone's view of what beauty is for men and women!

Some beauty trends are relatively harmless—like the popularity of a certain hairstyle or body piercing. But, once society puts pressure on people to strive for something they will never attain naturally, only negative results will follow.

There's absolutely nothing wrong with having surgery to be more confident. The issue is in the expectation to meet someone to make you happy after doing so. No one can make you happy. You find happiness first, then whoever you meet should add to that happiness that already exists within.

Men will drool and gawk over you. Understanding the attention you will get is important. The reality is that sex is what will inspire men to go after you. Just keep in mind what you want and be ready to turn down a lot of "creeps." If dating and fun is what you want, then you'll have no trouble finding that.

If you want a long-lasting relationship, pay attention to what your potential partner says. Most people know how far a relationship will go from the beginning when they are dating someone. There are some people who don't know and they are willing to see how their connection can grow with a person. But, for the rest of us, we know what we're willing and not willing to compromise. Just trust your judgment. If you think someone isn't ready for a relationship based on their actions, then run! Do not stick around, set yourself up for disappointment and possibly heart ache.

Exaggerated Differences

"Do not set impossible goals for yourself; everyone is different."

It is no secret that men and women often have different preferences when it comes to relationships and partners. People should try to see past these differences and seek common ground. There are things that everyone can benefit from: stability, trust, compassion. When it comes down to it, the differences between what men and women really want in a relationship might not be all that different.

The problem is that there are aspects of society that exaggerate these differences. Certain ideas get amplified because they are catchy or interesting. A movie about a man and a woman who talk through their different desires and find a reasonable way to accommodate one another would probably not attract a wide audience. Likewise, an Instagram page of an everyday couple living an average life—working, shopping, raising kids, walking their dog—would likely never achieve great popularity compared to a profile that focuses on hyper reality.

Think about how many sexualized images of women are on social media compared to the number of pictures of everyday women going about their business of normal life. Even women have this idea now that if they work out, they can look like certain Instagram models who have had butt and breast surgery. Just because people work out in an Instagram video, that doesn't mean that they worked out to get the shape they have. Do not set impossible goals for yourself; everyone is different. We all have different body types so what may look great on one person might not be great for you and vice versa. Along with that, what might be achievable by you might not be attainable for someone else. We all have to strive to be the best version of ourselves.

Perhaps there are women out there who used to want a stable relationship with a kind guy. After years of social media indoctrination, now they want a relationship with a jet-setting playboy. Perhaps there are men out there who once fantasized about a woman who could take care of them, cook a good meal, listen to his problems and share his burdens. Now all he wants is an over sexualized, hyper reality woman. How is this good for anybody?

It is time to bring on the idea that it is perfectly fine for women to be comfortable and confident in who they are and what they want. Society has always put so much pressure on their appearance that even now some are still trying to attain the perfect butt, lips and breasts. In a way, it's like the men have shown what catches their attention and now it's what most women focus on, convinced that it is beautiful and sexy.

Achieving the Appearance You Want

"Will anyone even know what their kid will look like after a woman has undergone so much surgery?"

Health and fitness are valorized in our society today. It used to be that overweight people were the "attractive" ones. Being fat was a sign that you had wealth and power. This may seem strange to us today, but remember that the idea of beauty changes with time.

We also use the language of achievement to describe how people improve their appearance. If you work out regularly, improve your eating habits and live a disciplined lifestyle, then this is an achievement to be proud of. But what is a person achieving by getting plastic surgery, implants or using an Instagram filter on all their posts? Are any of these achievements to be proud of? No, but technology has outpaced society yet again. We still associate fitness and sexualized beauty as virtuous, good and healthy no matter how it is obtained. Likewise, we judge obese people harshly without a care for how they feel about themselves.

A person shouldn't take the drastic step of appearance-altering surgery without thinking long and hard about why they are doing it. Is it for the right reason? Some people are very uncomfortable in their own bodies. Surgery may be the best way to help them achieve lasting mental health.

If a person has surgery or goes on a crash diet, and the result is that they feel better about themselves, then great! But if what they *really* want is to turn heads and get more attention, there may be something deeply unhealthy and unsustainable at play. As we discussed at the start of this chapter, sexualized attention has very little to do with what is under the hood. It is skin deep and it never ever lasts. "Dick and dip" may be fun, exciting and boost a person's self-esteem, but most people will eventually want more.

Appearance as Empowerment

"Just be sure you are treated with respect and there is more to your relationship than just the way you both appear."

Feminist movements come and go, but at their core, they are all about empowerment. How should a woman be? What should a woman want? What does a woman need? More recently, people are asking the question, *"What does it even mean to be a 'woman'?"* Is it about sex? Gender? Appearance? Mindset? Motherhood? All of the above? Is it something ineffable that can never be identified?

Many people are rightly interested in these consequential questions of meaning and existence, but what impact do they really have on a person's day-to-day life? When a woman makes a decision on feminist grounds, is she doing it for herself or in service of a larger movement? When a man calls himself a feminist, is he just trying to seem "woke" or does he really care about the advancement of women in society? How much of "feminist" behavior is mere virtual signaling and how much is actually trying to make this a better society for women?

All these questions are beyond the scope of this book. The bottom line is every woman will define womanhood in her own way. For some, empowerment means working hard and building a career. For others, feminism means setting aside a career to raise children. After all, it takes the female reproductive system to make a child. For others, feminism means getting their appearance closer to today's ideal of feminine beauty. Others eschew society constraint and call that feminism.

At the end of the day, it is about personal choice and it certainly is not the place of a man to tell a woman what is or isn't "feminine," "womanly" or "empowering." If you are a man and the woman in your life makes a decision that doesn't sit right with you, try to understand their perspective. Make an effort to see how the action is empowering to them. Ask questions. Be a partner, not a bystander. Maybe they really are doing it for the wrong reasons. If so, you an still be part of the growth and process.

If you are a woman struggling to decide how to express your womanhood, consider your own needs and wants instead of what you think society demands of you. There are many ways to express femininity and womanhood and you are under no obligation to explain yourself.

The sexualization of the female body has always been an issue in human society. After all, the evolutionary purpose of any species is to procreate. It makes sense that so many men and women are preoccupied with appearances. As humans, we can also see past our primal instincts and assess how important they really are in today's society. Navigating the differences between what men and women want is part of the challenge of heterosexual relationships. It is unavoidable. If a couple is always kicking the can down the road and not facing the complexities of their desires, the relationship will eventually end. It is best to face these conflicts as they arise.

Some men will always jeopardize relationships for a physical feature that got their attention. Men are very visual creatures and the reasons why they cheat would be the greatest proof of that—if they were ever brave enough to admit it. They mostly cheat based on what they see. Women should feel confident in setting goals for how they want to look and be happy with their results. Most times, those procedures are based on body enhancements that are very sexualized alterations.

Women have been convinced that beauty is big lips, big boobs, and a big behind. Beauty is being packaged as an unreal goal derived from enhanced bodies. People that naturally have these features are blessed. But for someone to want to look like someone else seems extreme. If you have gotten surgery for yourself, you should feel comfortable with who you are. You may turn heads and get more attention than you've ever gotten before. But, please understand that it is sexual attention that you're receiving.

Now that you have undergone the procedure that accentuates your enhanced boobs and butt, men drool over you for that reason. What a catch-22! You had the procedure to be more confident and attractive. Now you have everyone's attention, but it's mainly sexual.

Sexual attention lasts as long as it takes until you've had sex with that person. Sometimes they even think of you as an accessory because of the way you look. We're all still human at the end of the day and when it's time to get to know each other, things are back to basics and it's less about how you look. "Just be sure you are treated with respect and there is more to your relationship than just the way you both appear."

If that person is visually and sexually driven, they will be gone no matter how much more there is to discover about you beyond your physical appearance. Make sure they are worth it. If you both just want sex, then that will work out rather easily with no issues.

Therapy

"Once you understand something, you can't be confused."

What is it like inside a snow globe?

You've probably seen this decoration many times in the winter. Maybe you have one on your shelf right now or buried in a box in the attic. Snow globes seem kind of magical—a whole little world captured in glass. When you shake it up, all you see is the peaceful, silent swirling of snow.

But what is it like inside?

Speaking literally, a snow globe isn't really full of snow, of course. Water, not air, is the medium through which the "snow" glitters and swirls. Think about what it might be like to be a figurine beneath that bulb of glass as the water sloshes around and the whole world shakes. Needless to say, being inside a snow globe and being the one who observes the snow globe are two very different experiences.

This is one of the core issues of romantic relationships, especially when partners live together. Your relationship can become your whole world, a small bubble where only you and your partner reside. Daily life may be full of ups and downs and you may even maintain a degree of spontaneity to keep things fresh.

However, everything is still happening *inside* the snow globe. It isn't possible, even under the most ideal circumstances, to see it from an outsider's perspective. This might not seem like a big deal until you think about the snow globe. What you experience on the inside isn't at all like what you might see from the outside.

Let's put it a different way. Why does a judge occasionally recuse themselves from certain cases? Usually, it is because they are closely associated with people or businesses involved in the case. This is known as *"conflict of interest."* Even if a judge is able to rule objectively and follow the letter of the law, they cannot avoid the *appearance* of a conflict of interest. For a ruling to be accepted, people need to have confidence that it is impartial. Without a perception of fairness, our entire legal system would fall apart.

The point is that you cannot accurately judge something from the inside. If you think you can—if you are a person who prides yourself on honesty and integrity—you need to take a good hard look at why you think you are an exception to this rule. The truly wise know that it is impossible to account for all personal biases and conflicts of interest when making decisions.

Help From the Outside

> *"Couples need to be able to step outside of themselves and look at their relationship objectively."*

Couples need to be able to step outside of themselves and look at their relationship objectively. They need to work together to assess and recognize the issues at play to deal with the conflicts that inevitably arise. Sure, it is useful—and necessary—to listen carefully to one another rather than placing blame. It is often said that there are two sides to every story—and with good reason. Placing blame feels good and because it feels good, people do it without even thinking.

But there are limits to resolving conflicts internally. You can talk to your partner until you are blue in the face about what is bothering you. You can spend hours explaining why you did—or didn't do—something that upset them. Sometimes, people just cannot hear one another. Judgment is clouded by emotion. Rationality gives way under the weight of anger and frustration. Never try to resolve a conflict when you or your partner are hungry or in a heightened emotional state. This is a recipe for disaster.

In moments like this, it is useful to have someone else to talk to. Partners in conflict with one another should seek the counsel of friends and family. With any luck, the friend or relative listens to their loved one blow off steam and helps them realize the fight wasn't that big of a deal after all. This might be a good strategy in the short term, but are these "venting sessions" really helping a person become a better partner? A more understanding partner? Some aren't fortunate to have such people in their lives who can listen and help alleviate the emotional stress of a conflict. What are these people supposed to do when they get into a fight with their spouse? There are no corners to retreat to in a snow globe.

The Professionals

"The important thing about counseling is that you don't need to be in a bad relationship to benefit from it."

The <u>marriage</u> counseling sector, which includes psychologists, counselors and therapists, is a $19 billion-per-year industry. By the law of supply and demand, there are clearly many couples who take advantage of this kind of professional help. There are two main types of professional help that couples seek: couples therapy and couples (or marriage) counseling.

Couples Counseling

This used to be known solely as "marriage counseling," but since people are marrying later in life, the umbrella term "couples counseling" is more accurate. A counselor is mainly focused on the here and now. They help couples understand their present relationship dynamics, both the healthy and the unhealthy ones. "The important thing about counseling is that you don't need to be in a bad relationship to benefit from it."

Many couples attend counseling before marriage. It is a great way to get things out in the open to ensure there are fewer surprises down the line. A good counselor will also teach conflict resolution skills. For a couple that rarely fights, an argument can be traumatic. Fear and mistrust can set in quickly, even if things have been great up to that point. Counseling helps prepare couples for the inevitable, even when things are great in the moment.

Counseling provides a neutral space where both partners can give up trying to control the situation. Stepping into a counselor's office is like stepping outside the snow globe of your relationship. You will benefit from the outsider's perspective and the way you process and react to that perspective will say a great deal about the kind of person and partner you are.

Couples Therapy

Couples therapy shares some characteristics with couples counseling, but there are a few important distinctions.

A therapist typically deals with the history of a relationship. The events, actions, choices and challenges that have led up to the present moment. They try to establish a common understanding of this history between the partners as a springboard for resolution. Couples may come to therapy with deep-seated resentment and conflict that are having a negative effect on one or both partners. Therapy can also be done together or separately. A therapist may want to meet with each partner alone in case they have trouble speaking freely in front of one another. As long as the therapist is seen as neutral, there is hope for dealing with the conflicts leading to a cycle of blame and harm.

Therapists, like counselors, will often emphasize the importance of communication. This may seem obvious, but if communication were easy, couples would argue a lot less. Depending on the person or the couple, therapy and counseling can be temporary or more long term. For some couples, a few months of counseling will do wonders, setting them up for possibly years of peace and pleasure. More deep-seated issues may take longer to resolve. Don't be afraid to start therapy or counseling if you think it'll help your relationship..

Reaching a Shared Understanding

"Both partners must be able to assess the relationship together and figure out what it needs to flourish."

Most people learn math, reading, writing and history in school. Hardly anyone learns how to communicate in a relationship, even though this is a skill that can make or break a person's happiness in today's world. For individuals who seek relationship longevity—and many people say they do—it is critical that you learn the social skills to communicate effectively.

Both partners must be able to assess the relationship together and figure out what it needs to flourish. When conflicts arise, most people will automatically blame the other rather than looking for a fault in themselves. This cycle needs to be broken for a relationship to succeed long term. Learn how to self-reflect. People are the way they are for many reasons. Much of this book has been spent building and acknowledging the understanding that many of these reasons are, at times, outside a person's direct control. However, this does not mean that person lacks agency.

If you want your relationship to work, you must be willing to adjust the way you operate. When it comes to communication, this can be exceedingly difficult. The way we speak, and the way we use language more generally, is deeply ingrained. It is pretty much beyond our conscious control most of the time. This means that changing the way we speak to each other is almost impossible without some outside help. We need constant reminders and frequent reinforcement. This is exactly the kind of help that counseling can provide if you and your partner always argue based on how you two may speak to each other.

Understanding this fact should make a person more compassionate and understanding towards their significant other. Counseling can get the ball rolling when it comes to changing bad behaviors or a damaging style of communication. When tension rises, however, people regress to their default behaviors. If you want to be with a person and you know they are trying to get better, it pays to be forgiving. They may be trying as hard as they can. If you do wait on them to come around, this doesn't mean you should wait forever. Set a timeframe for yourself.

Vicious Cycles

"When you're in a conflict, it is much harder to think whilst your emotions are in the mix."

Couples counseling is often beneficial, but it is not a panacea. There are no miracle cures that will prevent conflict and discord indefinitely.

If you and your partner do choose counseling, your attitude will make a difference before you even walk through the door. Expecting your partner to change overnight is an unrealistic expectation. You must also be willing to make the changes yourself if you haven't done so already. When you try to change a person and mold them to become more of what you want, the outcome will never satisfy you. Your partner may change their behavior in the moment, but demanding change without offering support is not a long-term fix. Unfortunately, this is a vicious cycle many couples fall into.

Let's say your spouse often neglects their chores and despite many reminders, they still don't follow through. You feel like you have no other option, so you raise your voice. Maybe you do something passive-aggressive, like slamming doors or cabinets, until you get their attention. Your partner responds by apologizing and doing their chores, but what about next time?

Do you really think that you've changed their behavior for good? As soon as they start neglecting their chores again, are you going to get angry again? How many times can this cycle repeat before your partner gets sick of you yelling and slamming doors? If this pattern seems familiar, you may be setting yourself up for a big fight in the future. You might be surprised when your partner finally gets sick of your passive-aggressive behaviors.

On the other hand, you may be less inclined towards this type of conflict. You might be the partner who suffers in silence instead of making your feelings known. In some ways, this is even worse than reacting in anger. If a lot of time goes by, and you've never told your partner how upsetting it is when they don't do their chores, it will be that much harder to reach a resolution. Your partner may be hurt or confused that you didn't speak up. They might be wondering what else you've been keeping inside. Staying silent can be a major breach of trust, although it's not as severe as cheating. Once that pattern is established, it can be very hard to break.

Be sure to read the earlier section, "Representatives," for a reminder about the difference between who people are inside vs. the person they show the world. If you never have hard conversations with your partner, you will never know if they are really who they claim to be. Everyone curates their appearance to the world, especially in the social media age. Counseling can help you learn if you and your partner are both showing your most honest selves to one another.

Many relationships go on far too long because one or both partners are afraid of revealing their true selves or desires. Even if neither of you go to counseling, being able to step out of the relationship mentally and look at it objectively will provide you both insight into what the issue is and how you both can improve. It'll be like asking a friend their opinion on your relationship. You both become the therapist of your own relationship.

Think of when you give advice. You are completely removed from the situation, so you are able to think logically and objectively about it. When you're in a conflict, it is much harder to think whilst your emotions are in the mix. If you both act as therapist in the way you assess your situation as a couple, the issue will be resolved much faster. It will take practice to think this way during a situation, but it will help tremendously.

A Theory of Change

"Figure out what is standing in the way of growth."

There are two competing schools of thought regarding how people develop. One school says that people never really change. Once they reach adulthood, their personality is set. This leads to the opinion that compatibility is the most important aspect of a relationship. If two people don't "naturally" match on some arbitrary set of criteria, there is no point in even trying. This results in people only choosing to date people in which they have a lot in common. The wisdom says, "These are the characteristics I want in a partner and if you don't check all the boxes, then bye-bye."

The other theory of human development is that people are continuously shaped by the world around them. Every choice, event and interaction changes a person just a bit. If you aren't growing, then you might as well be dying. People who believe this also place a high value on a person's agency— their ability to make choices that changes their circumstances. At its most extreme, this belief leads to the opinion that there is no single self. Who we are at any given moment changes is based on the context.

These two opposing views, however, can be reconciled. In fact, this book argues that they must be reconciled for an individual to maintain a lasting relationship that is mutually beneficial to all partners. People cannot change who they are inside, but they can control how they respond to the challenges of daily life with another person. Every behavior can be conditioned. Every habit can be altered. Every world view can be reshaped when new information is uncovered.

The caveat here is that some people are naturally more inclined to change. For some people, making meaningful changes is exceedingly difficult. This personality trait can be further exacerbated by mental health issues or drug abuse. If you are a person who has difficulty changing your routine, ask yourself why. Figure out what is standing in the way of growth.

There are many versions of yourself. Only close reflection and an open-minded viewpoint will help you discover the version that will be the best possible partner.

Think of any relationship that you had in the past. Think of your previous partner's personality, the good and the bad. Over the course of that relationship, they consistently stay true to who they were no matter what you did or how you tried to change them. If they were a jerk in the beginning, they were most likely a jerk in the end. It was just you choosing to "accept it and respect it" instead of letting them go.

People need to realize that the harder you try to change someone to be more tailored to what you want, the more obvious it should be for you to let them go. We are all fundamentally the same person we were years ago, but over time we become a different version of ourselves. Some people show who they truly are from the time you meet them to the time you leave them. When you first meet someone and you can clearly see that they are a jerk, "pack up your emotions and run the other way."

Dating Websites

"The very fact that people have always tried to make dating easier shows how difficult it can be to find someone for you."

Many people think that online dating is a new phenomenon, but the idea of computer-assisted partner matching is almost as old as the technology itself. In 1959, researchers at Stanford University fed data into an IBM 650, the most widely used computer of the decade, to match 49 eligible women with 49 eligible men.

For the next 40 years, until the advent of the World Wide Web, dozens of companies were founded with the explicit mission of using the latest technology to help people find love and commitment. The very fact that people have always tried to make dating easier shows how difficult it can be.

The next time you overhear someone bashing online dating, tell them to look up Happy Families Planning Services from 1959, Operation Match from 1965 or Great Expectations, the video dating service founded by Jeffrey Ullman in 1976. Ever heard of the Matchmaker Electronic Pen-Pal Network? Probably not, but the point is, for as long as we have been connected via the internet, we have tried to leverage its power to meet that special someone. The algorithms that powers today's dating websites and apps are more sophisticated than a video dating service or an online chatroom, but the central idea remains the same: It is possible to find love and companionship through virtual means.

Since apps and websites go in and out of fashion so quickly, it won't help to analyze the capabilities of each one. Instead, this chapter will take a close look at the intentions and circumstances that drive people to such services in the first place. Why might a person choose to date online or through an app?

Ease of Access

"It is simply easier, cheaper and faster to meet people online these days."

Technology makes life more convenient. The smartphone, in particular, puts the world at your fingertips. "It is simply easier, cheaper and faster to meet people online these days." In times of social distancing, it may be the only way to meet them. Some people go out to bars every weekend, spending thousands of dollars on drinks and hundreds of hours each year just to put themselves physically in a place where they hope to serendipitously meet that special someone. Compare that to the effort it takes to download a "free" dating app and build a profile. The savings are huge.

"Free" is placed in quotes here because nothing is 100% free. Developers make money by selling your data to advertisers hoping to leverage your time on the app as a way to get you to buy their products. There are many hidden costs of letting your data get sold to the highest bidder, but that is beyond the scope of this book. If you don't mind the trade-off, then again, online dating is cheaper and less time-consuming way to meet people.

Also, many apps make it all too easy to rapidly scroll through dozens of people in a single session without moving anything but your thumb. With a single swipe, you get that endorphin rush that comes with seeing a new face or an exciting body. Like much of dating, it all comes down to biology. You scroll until your body releases chemicals that activate the proper parts of your brain and there you have your match.

The downside is the part of you that gets excited by a pretty face or a great body is only one part of the puzzle. As many people have discovered, a matching profile doesn't necessarily lead to a lasting connection. Proponents of online and app-based dating will say that the profile and photos are just part of the possible attraction. It is up to the individual to decide how to move forward once they meet their potential new partner in person.

What's Missing From Dating Apps

"If online dating doesn't work, get out there and meet someone!"

On dating apps, what happens often is that, you have conversations with a lot of people but you may not meet them. But it speaks more to the fact that the app is good to meet new people but it doesn't necessarily mean you'll meet quality people or have a connection with anyone.

Dating apps seem to take serendipity and the spontaneity out of meeting people. It'll mostly be based on what you see and not entirely on how you feel. You might be curious to get to know them but there's less of a feeling because you're not interacting with them, you're sending a message and waiting on their response or you're liking their profile and waiting for a response. When you see someone that you do like in passing, by a chance encounter, that is a feeling that a screen cannot give you.

How many times have you gone clothes shopping online and saw something that looks nice but it didn't fit right when it arrived? It looks nice on a screen but the feel of it isn't there so how could you know if it'll be a final purchase? You don't!

Shopping for clothes online compared to shopping in person is not as great, as far as a final purchase. If you shop online, you can visit more sights and essentially come across more items but it's less of a guaranteed final purchase because you are lacking the in person experience. Online dating is no different. If you have a busy schedule, meet people online because you're busy and it's less time consuming. It doesn't matter how you initially meet someone whether it was in person or online. You still have to get to know someone in person. Meeting someone in person is the gateway to the next level. There still is no guarantee of having a connection, especially through an online dating service, but it's still worth trying if you really want to meet someone. "If online dating doesn't work, get out there and meet someone!"

Sexual Gratification

"If you are concerned that person is only into you because they want sex, ask!"

Today, many people associate dating apps with sex. Many dating apps have become glorified sex catalogs. While there is a subset of apps specifically designed to help people hook up rather than find lasting love, even the self-proclaimed dating services are often used to establish nothing more than physical connections.

All this simply means, to be a savvy user of a dating app, you must approach it with the right expectations. You have to ask the right questions. "If you are concerned that a person is only into you because they want sex, ask!" There is no harm in asking the question. If you're worried about chasing them away with an honest question, then it might be better to nip things in the bud. "It's OK if you lowered your expectations, but, your standards should remain high.

Dating apps and websites, especially those with a strong hookup culture, also present a problem for those in committed relationships. Yes! People in a relationship should stay clear from these platforms but they some how find a way to join, despite their commitment. They join out of FOMO and what seems to be trending in the social media culture. It has never been easier to ogle and communicate with other people. You don't even have to leave the couch. Dating apps make it quite easy to be picky, which, you should get who you want. Unfortunately, we may be turned off by the simplest things we see on someone's profile that pose no threat to the rest of a persons qualities. By clicking next, we may be missing a connection that could've blossomed into something great. This is the age of instant gratification at it's pinnacle, so far.

For this reason, partners should have clear expectations for one another when it comes to maintaining an active presence on a dating website or an app. You might consider yourself just a casual "lurker," but your partner may see such activity as a breach of trust. It is imperative, especially in today's interconnected world, that partners set ground rules when it comes to the use of such platforms.

If you are concerned about your partner using a dating app, you have all right to be. If you as the other partner feels it is your right to maintain a presence on a dating app, ask yourself why. Why do you think you need to scroll through images and profiles of other people while your partner is at work or even lying beside you in bed? What does that say about your level of commitment, loyalty, and integrity to them? Are you still sure you want to be in a committed relationship?

Playing the Game

"The media and the news that you consume can change the way you view yourself and the world."

For some people, dating is nothing but a pastime. Messaging other people doesn't mean anything serious. How many songs out there advocate that people pursue their own selfish wants? To act without care for the feelings of others? It isn't your fault that a person becomes attached. It isn't your fault that a person gets hurt or upset because you were living your best life, right? How can you be living your best life if all you are doing is spreading pain and mistrust?

The writer James Baldwin wrote that "he who debases others debases himself." To debase is to corrupt something or diminish its quality. When you create suffering for others, when you hold their feelings, needs and experience as less valid than your own, you are diminishing yourself. You are making yourself less worthy of love, companionship and happiness. Living a life free of compassion is not brave and it is not noble. Whenever you take advantage of someone, whenever you use someone, whenever you disregard your own moral compass, you are weakening yourself. You are hollowing yourself out and making yourself into a person that no reasonable person would want to be with.

The unfortunate reality is this: Dating apps and websites have made it easier than ever to debase yourself by debasing others. This is a lesson that many people learn, but only after a great deal of experience. Is it any wonder that so many people behave this way? When people hear a song that tells them to seek vengeance rather than understanding or to intentionally hurt people when things don't go your way, what is the natural outcome? I'll tell you. There will be a lot of people damaged and scarred from those relationships. That's what most, if not all, of those songs were based off of. It has been stated in this book before, but it bears repeating: The media and the news that you consume can change the way you view yourself and the world.

See the "Cheating" chapter for more about this damaging phenomenon.

How Open Is Too Open?

"This is me! Take it or leave it!"

Dating apps and websites encourage people to show the world certain parts of themselves while keeping other parts hidden at all costs. There has always been an element of gamesmanship to dating. Some people see it as a competition like chess or poker. Play your hand close, study each move carefully and always read between the lines.

A person is never supposed to be vulnerable, to discuss their fears or their past relationship failures. They aren't supposed to show the world their cracks. At the same time, people are told to be unapologetic about their flaws. They may even show pride around the times they cheated or lied. *"This is me! Take it or leave it!"*

But this is neither honest nor open. Being unapologetic about the things you cannot change is different from speaking honestly about your insecurities. It is OK to share a past mistake and tell a person that you wish things had gone differently. Regret should never rule your life, but it is impossible to feel regret sometimes. Talking to a potential new partner about your past mistakes sends the message that you care about personal growth and self-reflection and that you believe you are capable of being better. Many people find this growth mindset irresistible. Remember, you cannot change the whole trajectory of your life when you meet a new person. You can't hide years of damaging behaviors and missed opportunities. Not for long.

There is a fine balance between being guarded and being vulnerable. When getting to know someone online, don't feel pressured to tell them your whole life story. In fact, burdening people with your personal difficulties can actually be a form of control. Trying to draw sympathy and pity from someone makes it harder for them to be honest. If you paint yourself as just seconds away from a nervous breakdown, don't be surprised when people aren't honest with you. It is important to come across as a person who can handle the minor disappointments of daily life.

Because you Have Nothing Better To Do

"Dating apps become sex catalogs because you can easily pick and choose."

It is tempting to turn to a dating app when you are bored, but will anything good really come of this? Nothing is wrong with a "booty call," but don't expect it to turn into a lasting relationship, even if that is something you are seeking. Almost everyone seeks pleasure in the form of sexual gratification every now and then, but you still need to be upfront about that.

Also, keep in mind that time spent chasing a booty call is time you will never get back. If you want a lasting relationship, but months go by without finding one, you might be spending too much time seeking that quick fix. Young people, in particular, feel like they have all the time in the world, but when all is said and done, life is nothing but the choices you make and the people you experience moments with.

If your partner isn't doing certain things right or missing something to your standard, you can easily find someone else.

It sounds harsh, but it's a fact. When you can find someone so easily online, the person you're with becomes easily replaceable but if you replace them, you better be sure you're not making a mistake. "The grass is probably greener on the other side because you aren't taking the time to water, care and cherish your own." If you're even curious to meet new people, maybe you should just be single. Hopefully you value your partner enough and you're not interested in meeting new people.

"Dating apps become sex catalogs because you can easily pick and choose." You're choosing from a pool of millions of users. If you're willing to be a member of a dating app while you're in a relationship, then how much do you value your relationship and how much do you even value the people you're meeting on the apps knowing that they're easily replaceable? Seems like you're looking to find a replacement. If that's the case then break up with your partner before you start your search.

People are becoming unapologetic about who they are, as they should be. My fear is when unapologetic becomes uncompromisable. This will keep people from wanting a relationship. Women and men are headed towards a dynamic that lacks compassion. If they're not doing anything for you then they're a waste of time.

Some snicker about cheating on their partner, when they tell they're friends, as if it's something to be proud of. Some people are actually proud of cheating. No one wants to get hurt in any relationship, but it doesn't mean we should be ruthless towards one another. Communication is one of the most important components that goes into a relationship and it's a surprise that so many couples do not truly speak on how they feel, even though we all know communication is key.

That also means trust should be well regarded even when you're dating someone. If you can't trust your partner enough to tell them how you feel, then what kind of relationship is that? That doesn't have any hope to truly survive and be something beautiful. Communicate how you feel. State your fears, state your intentions, what's on your mind and be honest with each other.

If we all can't begin to do that, relationships will continue to fail. It's like a continuous poker game and you're going to bed with your rival that you sometimes have good times with or once had good times with. Why even bother staying together?

Experience Is What It's All About

"When the relationship does end, the most important thing is realizing what you have gained and how you've grown from it."

Like life, relationships are all about experience. We are taught that there is a "happily ever after." It is a beautiful idea and in stories, we smile at the thought of it. If you're like me, sometimes you even cry at those "happily ever after" moments.

Chemistry, growth and experience are the main factors that end relationships and the purpose of writing this book. All relationships will inevitably end but you can increase the life and length of your relationship by what you do day to day, with, and for, your partner.

When the relationship does end, the most important thing is realizing what you have gained and how you've grown from it. What have you learned? How have you grown? Are you a better version of yourself? Did you learn what not to do in future relationships? Did you help the person you were with? Did they help you? Did you experience a terrible relationship that you will never want to go through ever again? Was it a beautiful relationship that you can model your future relationships from, yet remove the parts of it that did not work so well?

"No matter the reason for a breakup, if someone does not want to be with you, at least you know." It's a blessing to know early on compared to being dragged through dirt and finding out the hard way that they weren't worth your time. Overall, you should be glad that you now know because no one should have to waste time looking for love and happiness or assuming they've already found it but in the end realize they haven't.

There are some relationships with couples that do not communicate well enough about how they feel. They live their lives in a routine that they don't want. They may get married and have kids together. The problem is only present when their kids witness their toxic relationship. If they are great parents, co-parenting is always the best way to handle that situation. Easier said than done, especially when you're co-parenting with someone you once loved. In most cases, both of you have zero to low tolerance for each other to the point that it's best not to even speak. But you must because it concerns the children.

If you're co-parenting, it can be a headache to make sure both parents are sharing the same effort. No matter what, one will always be doing more than the other. Hopefully, your significant other doesn't do so little that they're almost nonexistent. Most likely, whatever the effort your significant other gives during the relationship is the same amount they contribute when you have kids together.

Choose wisely on who you pick to share that experience with while also remembering that it'll end anyway if you both aren't keeping up with the relationship and putting in the effort it needs. So, before you have kids, remember, it's best you choose someone that you make a great team with vs. someone that just looks good! And please, do not get into a relationship because you feel lonely or you think you're at an age that you should settle down. This will only lead to the end of your partnership much quicker when you try to fit someone into your goals vs. meeting someone that you think is great for you.

In our society, a lot of the things we do are because of the pressures from what we see and what we're taught we should have achieved. When we are at a certain age, we should have accomplished certain things or be in a relationship, married and have a family. Living a life that you are pressured into will eventually make you feel like you're jailed and stuck in your own life. You subscribed to the idea that you should be this or that, which becomes your goal. Upon achieving that goal, you realize you've just blindly guided yourself to that. You succeeded, but you didn't actually want it. You just wanted to accomplish it and never questioned if that's what you wanted.

You may feel disappointed depending on how long you two have been together and how deep into the relationship you are. The key to life is experience and you should think of the relationship as a way that you have grown and learned, versus feeling heartbreak and disappointment. It may still be the ladder, but try to dwell on the fact that you've become a better version of yourself by what you have learned.

After you both finish explaining the way you feel, the resolutions are what show growth. Again, emotions make us all react impulsively. The "Therapy" chapter was about thinking and looking at your relationship objectively, assessing the situation together and coming up with the best solutions.

It is very difficult to step out of yourself mentally and objectively think about situations without emotion. But, if you can get better at it, it'll save you from a lot of arguments and frustration. Individual growth is continuously happening. When a relationship ends because of growth, both people should realize that it is not because of what either of them did. It is just time, a matter of time. We like to find out who was responsible for the relationship ending when we hear about a breakup. Was it your fault or theirs? This is not always the case. For a lot of long-lasting relationships, chemistry, growth and experience play a huge role in why the relationship ended.

People are continuously growing and evolving, so to think that you're going to be with someone forever is inaccurate. It is nice to hope for that and strive towards that and by doing so, you can extend the life of your relationship. But you will grow and might even be the one ready to move on eventually. Just because someone may be growing does not mean that they are better than you.

As mentioned in the "Growth" chapter, we are all creatures of growth and although we relatively stop growing physically, we never stop growing mentally and emotionally. When a relationship has naturally ran its course, what usually ends it is one partner, sometimes both, feeling like they have outgrown the relationship. This is the time when they may feel that they have grown apart. This is a result of human nature, not because either of them did anything wrong.

When we get used to an experience, we protest for change. You and your partner should be able to communicate the change you both want to happen. Most times, neither partner can step out of themselves and look at the relationship objectively and recognize the problem. It ends up being a very immature battle with a lot of emotions, pride, anger and frustration. Some couples may complete all the demands from their significant other, but we are who we are.

Eventually we will go back to our natural selves and habits and nothing is wrong with that as long as your partner knows that the change asked might not last permanently. If they expect that, then chances are they don't actually like you and the way you are. It's most likely time for them to move on.

A great question to consider when you're in a relationship or planning on getting into one is *"Do you like your partner?"* If you actually like the way they are and the way they think, your relationship will last. But if you don't and just focus on their looks or something else that makes you want to be with them, then there's a high chance the relationship will end much sooner.

Choose Wisely

"Focus on what you have learned."

When you don't actually like the one you're with, you will have no tolerance for them. When you have no tolerance for a person, you get annoyed of them. Because you're annoyed, you will have an attitude towards them. If things get to this point, the relationship is over and past due on its expiration date. Why be with someone that you don't like? There is no reason for it unless you are so selfish that you want them for yourself, but do not like them. Let them go their way so you both can have a real chance at finding someone better for both of you.

Also keep in mind that to make a relationship work, you have to satisfy your partner in things that they ask of you. Choose wisely! Its's either that you be who you are and hide your true self or be who they want you to be. There are times that you need to grow and be a better person. So, if you feel like them helping you change and it is healthy, then welcome that change and keep the relationship going.

But, if you know that change is toxic, completely non-representative of you and makes you feel uncomfortable, then let the relationship go because you'll never be what they want. At that point, if you stayed, you'll end up putting your happiness after the relationship. As stated in the "Happiness" section, this will only lead to the relationship ending sooner because you're not happy as an individual.

If even one partner in a relationship could look at the relationship from the outside looking in, many issues could be resolved or handled in a healthier way as explained in the "Therapy" chapter.

Experiencing a relationship is a part of living. Even though they all will end, the experience we gain from them is life-changing for better and unfortunately worse at times. But we all learn from them.

We might have experienced a relationship full of arguments and learned it is the type of relationship we do not want to be in. There might be a relationship that you lose the best of you by losing yourself in it, but now you've learned self-love and raised your standards of how you want to be treated by future partners. You might have also experienced a relationship in which you and your partner respected each other, but it naturally arrived at its end, due to the chemistry, growth and experience factors. It's OK because now you know what you want in your future relationships that will help it go as smoothly as you know it can. At times, we end up in very similar relationships like a vicious cycle that we can't escape.

It isn't until we experience a different relationship with a partner who loves differently and treats us completely better that we begin to know more about what we want in a relationship. The more relationships people have, the more they know what they want.

When relationships are coming to an end, it is always sad. The end of friendships and relationships are never easy. We dread not interacting with that person who has been such a big part of our lives. It's sad to think about. Rather than putting yourself through that big loss and trying to remedy that huge void, which by the way is nearly impossible, except with time. Focus on what you have learned.

You will find that there are so many lessons. The moments might have been a struggle to go through, but now in hindsight, you can see how you've grown as a person. There is also a bit of nostalgia in the thought process because when we think back, we realize we were gaining something valuable even though it might have been an argument, a disagreement or a compromise.

I am not against people being in a relationship, but I want people to realize that the experience, no matter when your relationship ends, is what lives on forever. Our emotions get the best of us, then we show our worst selves when we lose a significant other from a breakup because we may take it personally. But maybe your significant other has grown and wants to move on. It may or may not be because of you. No matter the reason, be happy they told you rather than being dragged on an emotional rollercoaster. But again, practicing thinking of your situation objectively will help you through it.

Experiences Last a Lifetime

"Honor and respect each other and there will be a 'happily ever after.'"

All relationships inevitably end, but experiences last a lifetime. Make your experience great every day. Extend the life of your relationship by doing what's best for it every chance you get. We all just want to be happy. Have some compassion. If you know you are not interested in being with someone, let them know as soon as you know so that they have a chance at being happy with someone else or by themselves. If you know you and your partner are right where you want to be, then be together. Honor and respect each other and there will be a "happily ever after!"

The End

Endnote Review Request:

If you enjoyed reading this book, please leave a review on your preferred platform such as Amazon, iBook, Nook, Google Play, Kobo, Audible, etc. Reviews helps other readers discover books like this.

You can also visit the authors social media profile and comment or start a conversation. Share your opinion whether you agree, disagree, had a favorite part or even if you've learned something.

Website: NolanBlake.net

Email: AuthorNolanBlake@gmail.com

Instagram: @AuthorNolanBlake

Facebook: https://www.facebook.com/people/Nolan-Blake/100072129016813/

Discord: https://discord.gg/gKZXEfAFzv

NFTs For Sale: https://opensea.io/NolanBlake

About the Author

Nolan Blake is a relationship coach that has helped many couples through tough times. He brings a unique and insightful perspective to our usual way of thinking. He has always had a passion for writing so coupled with giving advice, he has written this book to help people navigate through their romantic relationship and its many ups and downs. Nolan enjoys spending time exploring his creativity by developing storylines and philosophizing. If you can't find him, he's probably watching a period piece from the 1800s or in the gym.

www.ingramcontent.com/pod-product-compliance
Lightning Source LLC
Chambersburg PA
CBHW070900080526
44589CB00013B/1145